GODS WITH AMNESIA:
SUBTERRANEAN WORLDS OF INNER EARTH

Robert Sepehr

Printed in the United States of America

First Printing, 2016

ISBN 978-1-943494-07-1

Atlantean Gardens
5334 Lindley Ave #133
Encino, CA 91316

www.AtlanteanGardens.org

Table of Contents

Introduction

Where does the oxygen we breathe come from? Surface trees and rainforests are responsible for less than one-third of the Earth's oxygen, while marine plants, such as phytoplankton, are responsible for between 70 to 80 percent of the oxygen in the Earth's atmosphere.(1) While protecting the rainforest is a noble and worthwhile endeavor, which I support wholeheartedly, for the purposes of this book I felt it was important to establish that the vast majority of our oxygen comes from aquatic organisms. In other words, even in the unlikely scenario where every single tree were chopped down, we would still be able to breathe thanks to aquatic plant-life (ex. algae). The Earth has a tremendous amount of water, and these oceans, rivers, and lakes are teeming with numerous species of biologically active, oxygen-producing organisms.

There are more than 7,000 different species of algae, which come in three colors: red, brown and green.(2) Green algae get their color from chlorophyll, and thrive near the surface where there is the most sunlight for photosynthesis. Green algae are not as common as red and brown. Seaweed such as Kelp are not plants, but are actually algae. Brown algae is the most abundant, with over 5,000 species, though not all are totally brown. Red algae lives where light is dimmer, in deeper waters.(2)

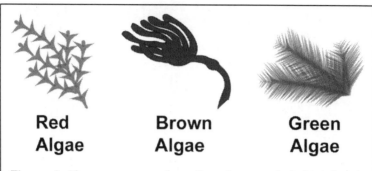

Red Algae   **Brown Algae**   **Green Algae**

Figure 1: Algae can range from the microscopic (microalgae), to large seaweeds (macroalgae) that grow over 100 feet long.

Discovered only in 1977, hydrothermal vents form when sea water seeps into the Earth's crust where it is heated by the underlying magma. It then rises to the surface, where it emerges through the seafloor as buoyant plumes of particle-rich, superheated fluid.(3) These vents lie hundreds to thousands of meters deep, and are home to a plethora of previously unknown species that thrive in extremely deep ocean ecosystems, which are commonly found near undersea volcanic chains. These deep sea hydrothermal vents are home to hundreds of species surviving at temperature extremes, and at pressures exceeding 200 times that on the Earth's surface.(3) How is life possible down there? In a process called chemosynthesis, microbes at the base of the food-chain convert chemicals from the vents into usable energy.

A prime example of chemosynthesis is in the warm fluids of the hydrothermal vent on the Juan de Fuca Ridge, near Washington state, rich with an exotic biodiversity of deep ocean life such as tube worms, limpets, and snails.(4) At 2200 meters (7200 feet) deep, where these animals live, there is NO SUNLIGHT, and thus no sun-driven photosynthesis. Life there thrives at high temperatures and pressures, extracting nutrients from a brew of chemicals dissolved from rocks below the seafloor. Bacteria are among the organisms at the base of the marine food chain and are plentiful around these vents where there is an abundance of nutrients.(5)

Figure 2: Juan de Fuca Ridge Hydrothermal Black Smoker

Before the discovery of these hydrothermal vents, and their ecosystems, scientists believed that only small animals lived at the ocean bottom, in seafloor sediments. They theorized that these animals received their food from above, because the established model of the marine food chain depended on sunlight and photosynthesis, just as the food chain on land does.(6) Mainstream academia taught that this was the only way life could survive in the darkness of the deep seafloor.

The discovery of hydrothermal vents changed all that. It became clear that vast communities of animals grew quickly and to larger than expected sizes in the depths without the aid of the Sun.(5) Instead of using light to create organic material (photosynthesis), microorganisms at the bottom of the food chain at hydrothermal vents used chemicals such as hydrogen sulfide (chemosynthesis).(4) At the seafloor, there are thriving ecosystems that receive energy not from the sun, but from the heat and chemicals provided by the planet itself. For many thousands of species dwelling in the deep, the energy to sustain life does not flow down from above, but comes up from the interior of the earth.

Since discovering hydrothermal vents in late 70's, researchers have identified more than 300 organisms with over 90% being completely new to science.(6) To live at the vents, many of these organisms have unusual and peculiar adaptations. Some scientists have speculated that life originated in deep environments, similar to these hydrothermal vents. Others have suggested that if these environments exist on other planets, then life might very well exist there too.(7)

Figure 3: Unidentifed seaspider from Juan de Fuca ridge hydrothermal vents (2300m)

In a May 2015 article in the *Science Times,* called "NASA Hopes to Rely on Algae and Bacteria for Oxygen Production on Mars", Rachel Went details how one of the most critical issues in colonizing Mars, oxygen production, may be solved by two very basic organisms: bacteria and algae:

"NASA envisions biodomes, stretching across the Martian landscape, which would house vast colonies of oxygen-producing algae and bacteria. But first they'll see if it works on a small scale. They intend to send tightly sealed canisters of microorganisms aboard future rover missions that would then be implanted in the Martian soil. The canisters will then be monitored, hopefully resulting in the production of oxygen. And their concept is hardly science fiction. For these miniscule organisms have been performing this vital function on Earth for millions of years. Between 70 and 80 percent of the oxygen on our planet is generated by photosynthetic algae and cyanobacteria. Algae contain light-absorbing chloroplasts and produce oxygen through photosynthesis. They can be found in fresh and saltwater, and on rocks, trees, and in soil. Cyanobacteria are also aquatic and photosynthetic and make up the oldest known fossils on Earth: the 3.5 billion-year-old stromatolites that dot the shallow shores of Western Australia. These organisms are part and parcel to life on our planet. And considering the fine job they do here on Earth, perhaps they can do the same for Mars."(8)

Figure 4: Artistic concept of NASA's Martian Greenhouse

Phytoplankton are microscopic, and usually inhabit the top layer of oceans and bodies of fresh water. Most phytoplankton float, preferring to reside near the surface where light penetrates the water. At certain times and places, they can reach a hundred meters (about 100 yards) in thickness. Phytoplankton, kelp, and algae produce oxygen as a byproduct of photosynthesis, a process which converts carbon dioxide and light into sugars which are then used for energy. While the process of photosynthesis usually implies the presence of sunlight, the Sun is not the only available light or energy source able to power photosynthesis, which we will explore later.

In the context of an underground cave, or a deep subterranean cavern, one could expect to find plenty of oxygen if there was a sufficient water source with the right conditions near by. Recently, geologists established that there is more ocean water below the surface, than there is above the Earth's crust.(9) According to a 2014 article published in *Nature World News,* entitled "Vast Underwater Ocean Trapped Beneath Earth's Crust":

"Scientists have discovered evidence of a vast water reservoir trapped hundreds of miles beneath the surface, capable of filling Earth's oceans three times over."(9)

Although a considerable amount of this subterranean water is trapped within the molecules of rocks, there is still a tremendous quantity of life sustaining liquid water which flows deep beneath us.

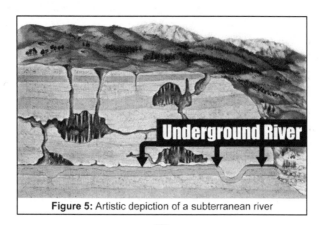

Figure 5: Artistic depiction of a subterranean river

It is amazing how the dark depths of caves harbor some of the most mysterious, bizarre, and beautiful animals yet discovered. *LiveScience* published an article in 2012 called *Cave-Dwelling Plants: Strange Subterranean Nettles Discovered In China,* describing massive caves recently discovered in China that contained unusual new species of plants that require very little light to photosynthesize.(10) These new plant species were described in the *journal PhytoKeys*:

*"One might not expect flowering plants with pinkish petals to be flourishing on the floor of a dark cave, but that's exactly where researchers discovered such a species in southern China. Botanist Alex Monro, of London's Natural History Museum, said he thought his Chinese colleague must have been mistranslating a word when he first mentioned the cave-dwelling plants. But then Monro saw the flora for himself. "When we stepped into our first cave, Yangzi cave, I was spellbound. It had an eerie moonscape look to it and all I could see were clumps of plants in the nettle family growing in very dark condition[s]," Monro said in a statement. The newly described plant was dubbed Pilea cavernicola. While it doesn't grow in total darkness, **it survives with levels of light as low as 0.04 percent of full sunlight in caves** in China's Guangxi province, the researchers said."(11)*

In *The biology of caves and other subterranean habitats,* David Culver and Tanja Pipan provide an updated clarification and synthesis of our understanding of the biology of the subterranean world.(12) In it, we learn that the heat from deep sea vents is high enough that VISIBLE light is emitted.(13) Over 94% of the world's unfrozen freshwater is stored underground, compared to only 3.6% found in surface lakes and reservoirs (14), with the rest in soil, rivers and the atmosphere. The authors make the case for 521,000 square kilometers of subsurface spaces and cavities in the bedrock of the United States alone.(12) Most of these contain water which means that roughly 10-40% of the total prokaryotic biomass (ex. bacteria) on the planet may be in the subsurface. It is very interesting to consider the many microorganisms that can and do can obtain energy from the chemical bonds of inorganic molecules.(15)

It is equally fascinating how some organisms, such as bacteria or algae, can produce light, or glow in the dark. The word for this seemingly magical ability is called "bioluminescence," which comes from "bio," meaning life, and "lumin," meaning light. Most of these plankton glow blue, but a few glow red, green, or orange. Some tiny animal plankton (zooplankton) are big enough to see with the unaided eye. Most bioluminescent zooplankton don't glow in the dark themselves, but instead squirt globs of glowing chemicals into the water. Some zooplankton use bioluminescence to attract a mate, or to form reproductive swarms.(16) Not only is nature's biochemistry fascinating, it can also be extremely beautiful, especially given the backdrop of a dark, misty cave.

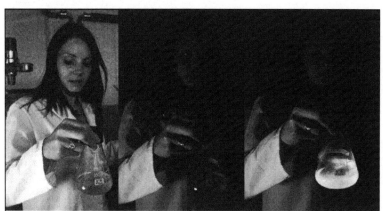

Figure 6: Dr. Charlotte Marcinko of the National Oceanography Center triggers chemical reactions in bioluminescent organisms

Glowing bacteria can live alone, or with other organisms, such as fish and squid, dwelling inside their organs in a symbiotic relationship, or as parasites. Alone, the bacteria doesn't glow that much, but in large enough colonies something amazing happens, called quorum sensing. The bacteria, upon realizing they have enough of each other around, activate genes that allow them to glow. The light emitted is extremely efficient, at around 99%, meaning that only 1% is lost through heat, thus producing a luminescence that is also cool.(16)

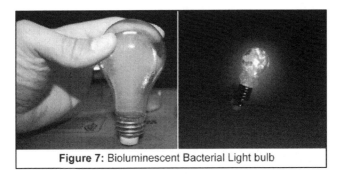

Figure 7: Bioluminescent Bacterial Light bulb

Glow worm is the common name for various groups of insect larvae and adult larviform females that glow through bioluminescence. They may sometimes resemble worms, but are actually insects. The glow they produce, through by a chemical reaction, is incredibly efficient; nearly 100% of the energy input is turned into light (Compare this to the best light-emitting diodes at just 24%). The purpose of the glow varies. Adult females may glow to attract a male for mating. Some types of larvae are believed to glow as a warning to predators not to eat them, as they are sometimes toxic. The Arachnocampa and Orfelia larvae, on the other hand, glow to attract prey into sticky snare lines, which capture the pray for the larva to feed on. Australia and New Zealand have some of the most spectacular caves, where one can go on guided tours to witness this natural phenomenon up close.

Figure 8: Waitomo Glow Worm Caves, New Zealand

Some winged beetles are more commonly called fireflies, or lightning bugs, for their conspicuous use of bioluminescence during twilight to attract mates or prey. The light produced by fireflies is also a "cold light", with no infrared or ultraviolet frequencies. It is the result of a chemical reaction emitted from their lower abdomens, and may be yellow, green, or pale red, with wavelengths from 510 to 670 nanometers.(17)

Why do some mushrooms emit light? Making light isn't common in fungi; scientists have described about 100,000 fungal species, and only 75 glow.(18) The question of glowing mushrooms dates all the way to Aristotle, who is the first person known to have wondered about this, according to Jay Dunlap, a geneticist and molecular biologist at the Geisel School of Medicine at Dartmouth College. In the March 2015 journal, *Current Biology*, Dunlap reported on experiments that suggest at least one kind of mushroom controls when it glows. Neonothopanus gardneri is the name of this dramatic mushroom, which commonly grows in Brazilian forests and emits an eerie green light.

Figure 9: Luminescent (Glow-in-the-Dark) Mushrooms from a Forest in Sao Paulo, Brazil

Lab work has shown that the glow of this particular mushroom did not happen randomly or by accident.(18) Scientists found that these mushrooms made light mostly at night, so experiments were conducted to determine why. The findings indicated that the mushrooms lured bugs, which then spread the mushroom's spores where there was very little or no wind.(19) Of the 75 currently known species of bioluminescent fungi, almost all are mushroom-forming, white-spored, and members of the order Agaricales (Basidiomycota). Bioluminescent fungi emit a greenish light at a wavelength of 520–530 nm of continuous light emission which occurs only in living cells and may occur in both mycelia and fruit bodies.(19) Conditions that affect the growth of fungi, such as pH, light and temperature, have been found to influence bioluminescence, suggesting a link between metabolic activity and fungal bioluminescence.(20) According to studies, in dark environments, bioluminescent fruit bodies may be at an advantage by attracting insects and other arthropods that could help disperse their spores.(21) If this conclusion holds, one could reasonably hypothesize that environments with little or no wind, such as deep subterranean caverns, could potentially harbor an especially high proportion of luminescent fungi.

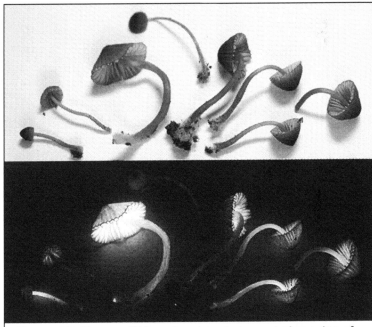

Figure 10: Mycena Chlorophos is a documented species of bioluminescent fungi from the Bonin Islands off Japan's coast

In the poem "The Ancient Track," by H. P. Lovecraft, fox-fire is seen glowing in field and bog where the narrator is convinced he will find the town of Dunwich.(22) In the novel *The Adventures of Huckleberry Finn*, by Mark Twain, Huckleberry Finn and Tom Sawyer use foxfire as a light source while digging a tunnel.(23) Fox-fire, sometimes also called "fairy fire", is the bioluminescence present in a fungus usually found in decaying wood. The oldest recorded documentation of foxfire is by Aristotle, in 382 B.C., whose notes refer to a light that, unlike fire, was cold to the touch. The Roman thinker Pliny the Elder also mentioned glowing wood in olive groves. In the forests of the Congo, this glowing fungus is known as "chimpanzee fire", and is responsible for breaking down much of the decaying leaves on the forest floor.

Figure 11: Scientists hypothesize that the bright bluish-green light is meant to attract insects that help spread fungal spores.

A lichen is a composite organism that arises from algae and cyanobacteria, living in a symbiotic relationship among filaments of a fungus; the algae feeds the fungus.(24) Fungi are incapable of making their own food. They usually provide for themselves as parasites or decomposers. The combined life form has properties which are very different from the properties of its component organisms. Lichens come in many colors, sizes, and forms, often having a greenish, gray, yellow, brown, or blackish thallus, which grows in leaf-like, crust-like, or branching forms on rocks or wood. Lichens aren't luminous, but they can glow because of the chemistry of the symbiotic relationship involved.(25) An example of the intensity and practicality of this luminescence comes from the first World War, where soldiers in the trenches supposedly fixed chunks of the glowing wood to their helmets and bayonets to avoid nasty accidents at night.

Out of the 20,000 or so lichen species, only two are poisonous: Letharia vulpina and Vulpicida pinastri, or Wolf Lichen and Powdered Sunshine Lichen.(25) Both of these are conveniently yellow. Some lichen are edible, but require proper preparation to be eaten.(26) Unprepared lichen tastes somewhat bitter, and probably won't kill you, but can be unpleasant on your digestive track.

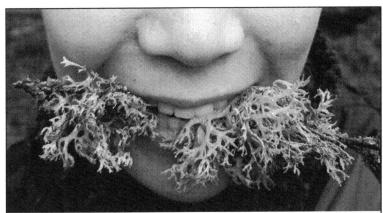

Figure 12: Lichens are abundant, widespread, and many species are edible and very rich in starch-like substances

One of the most widespread and commonly eaten lichen is Cladonia rangiferina, also known as Cladina rangiferina, which can also be made into an alternative to grain alcohol, and has even been made into molasses. Most lichen that you see are roughly 94% carbohydrates, which is about 14% more carbohydrates than a potato. To make this nutrition source usable, one must first remove the acid, which is what makes digestion difficult. The amount of acid varies from species to species with the Cladonias being among the the least acidic. Nutritional studies suggest Cladonias are, by dry weight, 1.4% ash, 5.4% protein, 32.9% fiber, 2.1% fat, 0.501% niacin, 3.7% calcium, and 0.09% phosphorus. They also have vitamin A, fiber, and protein.(26)

To make the lichen edible they are soaked in several changes of water, or with hardwood ashes. The modern version is to soak them in a 1% solution of potash. A method used in China is to boil lichen for 30 minutes, then soak them for two days in several changes of water, and then they are finally steamed. They are then ready to eat, plain or mixed with other things, or dried and added to flour or as a thickener to soups.(26)

Lichen is often cooked until it turns into a gelatinous mass. The longer you soak and boil them, and the more frequently you change the water, the more palatable and less acidic they will be.(26)

One final word on the edibility of lichen. Noma, a Danish restaurant in Copenhagen that serves moss and lichen as a delicacy, has for three consecutive years (2010, 2011 and 2012) won the annual S. Pellegrino World's 50 Best Restaurant Awards.(27) Noma currently charges around $100 for a three-course dinner, featuring exotic dishes such as the protein-rich "Deep fried reindeer lichen with mushroom powder". Yum!

Figure 13: Fluffy tangles of reindeer lichen and seaweed-like Icelandic moss steamed and then deep fried to a fragile crisp

We have briefly considered the possibility of how one may potentially have access to water, breathable air, an underground food source, and also have at least some minimal degree of diffuse visibility in a deep, dark subterranean cave system, tunnel or cavern. Now, let us proceed to chapter one.

Chapter 1

In his 1885 book called *Paradise Found: The Cradle of the Human Race at the North Pole,* William Fairfield Warren placed Hyperborea, as well as Atlantis, Eden, Mount Meru, Yggdrasil and Avalon, in the Arctic region.(28) He was convinced that the Garden of Eden itself was at the North Pole. Warren proposed that all these fabled lands that are now mostly remembered as mere myth: they are folk memories of a far northern domain, inhabited long ago, and from which civilization first emerged and then diffused south.

Following in the footsteps of Homer, Virgil and Hesiod, Warren placed the primordial Titan Atlas of Greek mythology, or his world pillar, at the "ends of the Earth", meaning the far northern arctic regions. He equated Atlas, who supported the Heavens on his shoulders (or the earth on a pillar), with the Atlas described by Plato as the first ruler of Atlantis.(29)

Figure 14: William Fairfield Warren (1833 – 1929)

In Warren's view, all the axis mundi of ancient legends (world axis, world tree, Yggdrasil, Irminsul or Atlas' pillar) had to be in the far north "at the top of the world":

"To locate these in right mutual relations, one must begin by representing to himself the earth as a sphere or spheroid, and as situated within, and concentric with, the starry sphere, each having its axis perpendicular, and its north pole at the top. The pole-star is thus in the true zenith, and the heavenly heights centering about it are the abode of the supreme god or gods."(28)

Bal Gangadhar Tilak was a very important and revered spiritual and political leader of India from 1880 to 1920. He was also a mathematician, astronomer, historian, journalist, and philosopher. In his book, *The Arctic Home in the Vedas*, written at the end of 1898 and first published in March 1903, Tilak theorized that the North Pole was the original home of Aryans, during the pre-glacial period, and that they had to leave due to the ice deluge.(30)

Figure 15: Bal Gangadhar Tilak (1856 - 1920)

In support of his theory, Tilak points to certain Vedic hymns, Avestic passages, Vedic chronology and Vedic calendars, which all describe ancient Aryan migrations from the Arctic to northern Europe and Asia, in search of lands for new settlements.(30)

Tilak cites *Paradise Found or the Cradle of the Human Race at the North Pole* as sharing his perspective to a great extent. Warren dedicated his book to Prof. Max Muller of Oxford University, and Tilak shared his ideas with Prof. Muller just before he passed away. All of these men shared the view that further study of Vedic hymns and Avestic passages reveals the long journey of primitive Aryan antiquity in the North.

Numerous Vedic hymns and Avestic passages record characteristics of the ancient Aryan Arctic home. They come down to us, interpreted sometimes as descriptions of the prevailing conditions, and sometimes as mere myths. *The Arctic Home in the Vedas* has been cited in the works of Julius Evola, Savitri Devi, Rene Guenon, Jean Haudry, and John G. Bennett. In the words of Bal Gangadhar Tilak:

"It followed, therefore that if the Vedic evidence pointed to an arctic home, the forefathers of the Aryan race must have lived therein not

after but before the last Glacial epoch. But the traditions preserved in the Avesta dispense with the necessity of relying on geology for this purpose. We have now direct traditional evidence to show [1] that the Airyana Vaejo had originally a good climate, but Angra Mainyu converted it into a winter of ten and a summer of two months, [2] that the Airyana Vaejo was so situated that the inhabitants of Yima`s Vara therein regarded the year only as a day, and saw the sun rise only once a year, and [3] that the happy land was rendered uninhabitable by the advent of a Glacial epoch which destroyed all life therein."(30)

◇◇◇

According to Tilak, after the destruction of the original Arctic home by the last Ice Age, the Aryan survivors roamed the northern parts of Europe and Asia in search of lands suitable for new settlements. Tilak calls this the Pre-Orion Period, when the vernal equinox was in Orion. Many Vedic hymns can be traced to the early part of this period. The Pre-Orion Period was followed by the Krittika Period, when the Vernal equinox was in Pleiades. Traditions about the original Arctic home had grown dim by this time and were often misunderstood. The Pre-Buddhistic Period followed, when the Sutras made their appearance.

Turning to the latest geological evidence, the last Glacial period closed and the Post-Glacial Period commenced around 8,000 BC, or about 10,000 years ago.(31) There were at least two Glacial, and one Inter-Glacial, periods. The geography of land and water on the earth during the Inter-Glacial period was quite different from what it is today. The coming of the Glacial age destroyed the genial climate and rendered the regions unsuited for habitation by tropical plants and fauna.(31) One needs only to examine the flash frozen carcasses of mammoth found in the arctic, with still undigested semi-tropical vegetation in their stomach (plants which can no longer be found in the arctic) to understand that the climate changed very abruptly, and catastrophically as far as the habitation was concerned.(32)

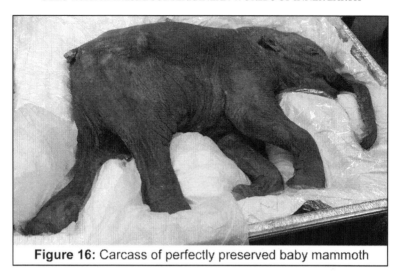

Figure 16: Carcass of perfectly preserved baby mammoth

Raymond Bernard's book *The Hollow Earth*, relays an entertaining story regarding an Arctic discovery (33), from a doctor who reports that one of his patients, a man of Nordic descent, told him the following:

"I lived near the Arctic Circle in Norway. One summer my friend and I made up our minds to take a boat trip together and go as far as we could into the North country. So we put a months worth of food provisions in a small fishing boat and set to sea. At the end of one month we had traveled far into the north, beyond the Pole and into a strange new country. We were much astonished at the weather there. Warm, and at times at night it was almost too warm to sleep.

"Then we saw something so strange that we were both astonished. Ahead of the warm open sea we were on what looked like a great mountain. Into that mountain at a certain point that ocean seemed to be emptying. Mystified, we continued in that direction and found ourselves sailing into a vast canyon leading into the interior of the Earth. We kept sailing and then we saw what surprised us... a Sun shining inside the Earth.

"The ocean that had carried us into the hollow interior of the Earth gradually became a river. This river led, as we came to realize later,

all through the inner surface of the world from one end to the other. It can take you, if you follow it long enough, from the North Pole clear through to the South Pole. We saw that the inner surface of the Earth was divided, as the other one is, into both land and water. There is plenty of sunshine and both animal and vegetable life abounds there. We sailed further and further into this fantastic country, fantastic because everything was huge in size as compared with things on the outside. Plants are big, trees gigantic and finally we came to Giants. They were dwelling in homes and towns, just as we do on the Earth surface, and they used a type of electrical conveyance like a mono-rail car, to transport people. It ran along the river's edge from town to town.

"Several of the Inner Earth inhabitants, huge Giants, detected our boat on the river, and were quite amazed. They were, however, quite friendly. We were invited to dine with them in their homes, and so my companion and I separated, he going with one giant to that giant's home and I going with another giant to his home. My gigantic friend brought me home to his family and I was completely dismayed to see the huge size of all the objects in his home. The dinner table was colossal. A plate was put before me and filled with a portion of food so big it would have fed me abundantly an entire week. The Giant offered me a cluster of grapes and each grape was as big as one of our peaches. I tasted one and found it far sweeter than any I had ever tasted outside. In the interior of the Earth all the fruits and vegetables taste far better and more flavorsome than those we have on the outer surface of the Earth.

"We stayed with the Giants for one year, enjoying their companionship as much as they enjoyed knowing us. We observed many strange and unusual things during our visit with these remarkable people, and were continually amazed at their scientific progress and inventions. All of this time they were never unfriendly to us, and we were allowed to return to our own home in the same manner in which we came... in fact, they courteously offered their protection if we should need it for the return voyage."(33)

Figure 17: Sailboat seen through huge iceberg cave

Another account of a fantastic subterranean journey into the inner world through an opening in the Arctic region, appeared in *A Voyage to the Inner Earth*.(34) This novel, also published as the *Smoky God*, was first released in 1908, and presented as the true account of Olaf Jansen, a Norwegian sailor, who along with his son discovered a northern entrance to the Earth's interior.

They lived inside unimaginably gigantic caverns deep inside the Earth for two magnificent years, as guests of the inhabitants of an underground network of subterranean colonies or cities, who ranged in height from 10 to 12 feet tall.(34) Their capital city was also said to be the original Garden of Eden, and had everything one would expect from a place regarded as a Biblical paradise: a beautiful oasis deep under the crust, with flowing rivers, fruit trees and vegetation, and with a soft diffuse glow which kept the massive caverns perpetually lit.

In the story, the primary source of subterranean light came from an artificial sun which never set.(34) This explanation conveniently provided a way for enough luminescence for photosynthesis to take place, resulting in a plausible ecosystem underground. An artificial Sun, however, is far from the only source of light one can expect to find, even many miles, below the Earth's surface.

Can there actually be light below the surface of the Earth, enough to sustain plant life, without any exposure to the Sun? The answer is YES. As I pointed out in the introduction, bio-luminescent organisms have the ability to produce light (glow), almost like magic. Chinese chemists have recently reported that, in the absence of sunlight, bioluminescence can effectively drive photosynthesis.(35) Hiroshi Imahori, an expert in biomimetic systems for artificial photosynthesis at Kyoto University in Japan, says in regards to his teams research:

◇◇◇

"Photosynthesis is one of the most important processes for life on Earth. However, photosynthesis is strongly dependent on the light source and extreme conditions will limit photosynthetic activity. This study has successfully demonstrated the potential utility of bioluminescence as a light source for photosynthesis."(35)

◇◇◇

It has now been conclusively demonstrated in laboratory conditions that photosynthesis from a bioluminescent source exhibits an extremely high rate of energy conversion efficiency.(35) In general, plants grown under a blue light spectrum from light emitting diodes (LEDs) and fluorescent lamps photosynthesize much faster than plants grown under a red or green light spectrum. This faster rate of growth is also exhibited with the photosynthesis that takes place from the blue-green glow emitted by bioluminescent organisms that were tested.(35)

Bioluminescent organisms can use their natural ability to produce light to trick predators, to attract mates and even to communicate.(36) The diversity of creatures with this ability is as astonishing as it is beautiful, from algae and the common firefly to deep-sea dwellers that are rarely seen by humans. Many of these creatures are not closely related, and their bio luminescent traits have seemingly evolved separately, at least 30 times.(36)

With a seemingly never ending, Swiss cheese-like network of semi-lit subterranean caves and glowing underground caverns, it makes one wonder what could be dwelling in the vast unexplored areas under the crust.

"Smoky God" is the name given to the artificial sun situated in the center of the Earth, in *A Voyage to the Inner Earth.(34)* If there is any truth to the story of Olaf Jansen and the Smokey God "far beyond the North Wind", then what route could they have stumbled upon to reach the earth's interior paradise? Do any maps depict the Arctic sea as anything other than covered with snow and ice?

A map originally published in 1570, by Abraham Ortelius of Amsterdam (1527-1598), is called the Theatrum Orbis Terrarum, and is considered to be the first true modern atlas. The north polar inset map (actual size 7 cm in diameter) presents a central continent of Hyper Borei (Hyperborea) at the Arctic region.(38) Many of the maps in this atlas maps were based upon sources that no longer exist or are extremely rare.

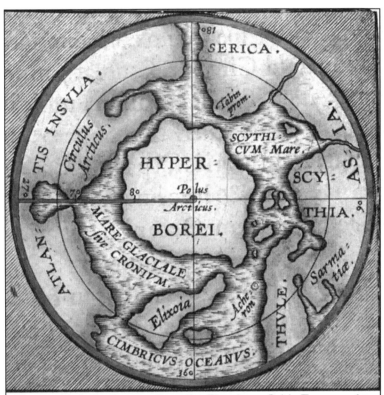

Figure 18-1: Arctic map from the Theatrum Orbis Terrarum by Abraham Ortelius (1570) depicts "Hyper Borei" as an island in the far North, and is considered as the first true modern atlas.

Mercator's maps were among the earliest to display the Arctic as a composition drawn from Classical and Nordic sources.(37) Gerardus Mercator (1512-1594) was a cartographer and mathematician born in what is now Belgium. He developed the Mercator projection world map, which is still in use today.

Figure 18-2: Gerardus Mercator (1512-1594)

Mercator left us his map from the Sixteenth Century, the first to offer an image of the Arctic as sourced from a now lost Fourteenth Century book, the *Itinerarium* of Jacobus Cnoyen.(37)

Cnoyen himself had two main sources: another now lost book, *Inventio Fortunatae*, and yet another now lost book, the *Gestae Arthuri*.(37) The most distinctive map feature is located directly in the center; four large islands appear where the Arctic Ocean should be.

Figure 19: Mercator's 1569 Map of the Arctic

Such a large, exposed landmass likely does not exist today (as depicted), but remnants of it might. What Mercator and other cartographers of his time were showing, probably unknowingly, was an Arctic landmass that existed there many thousands of years ago in Antediluvian times. The back of the map gives insight about a land called Bjarmia or Bjarmaland. It's location is described as:

"An extreme region of the North whose apex in the firmament is the North Pole. For this reason, half of the year is one and the same miraculous day, the other half continuous night.

"In Bjarmia, there are mountains covered by eternal snows untouched by the heat of summer, forests without trails, rare animals, and roaring rivers within the abysses of crags. Strange tribes also reside there, and it is known that an immeasurably rich forest troll named Memming has lived at one point in Bjarmia.

"The way to these creatures is so filled with insuperable difficulties that a mortal has a difficult time getting there. The largest part of the journey is cloaked with an incredibly deep layer of snow: anyone intending to traverse it must use a conveyance pulled by harnessed reindeer."

According to Valery Uvarov, in *The Second Birth of Hyperborea*, Mercator is actually depicting northern Labrador as Greenland, claiming that Greenland itself was originally part of the true Hyperborea.(39) Interestingly, on the back of the Mercator map a legend reads:

"The waters of these 4 arms of the sea were drawn towards the abyss with such violence that no wind is strong enough to bring vessels back again once they have entered; the wind there is, however, never sufficient to turn the arms of a corn mill."

Very similar words are related by Giraldus Carnbrensis in his book on the marvels of Ireland. Thus he writes:

"Not far from the isles (Hebrides, Iceland, etc.) towards the North there is a monstrous gulf in the sea towards which from all sides the billows of the sea coming from remote parts converge and run together as though brought there by a conduit; pouring into these mysterious abysses of nature, they are as though devoured thereby and, should it happen that a vessel pass there, it is seized and drawn away with such powerful violence of the waves that this hungry force immediately swallows it up never to appear again".(37)

Just as Plato wrote about the "mythical" Atlantis, a continent which was said to be once located above sea level in the Atlantic, Herodotus wrote about the legendary Hyperborean continent which he said once existed in the far North.(40) This map not only depicts what could very well be the remnants of Hyperborea, but it also seem to imply that a race of Pygmies once heavily populated the northern Canadian and Arctic regions where these four rivers intersect.

Written on the map, Mercator explains that the ocean waters rush inward towards the center, between the islands, to the pole, where they plunge deep into the Earth.(37) Directly at the pole is a black island 33 leagues in circumference. The converging four rivers are rumored to be, at least partially, driven by powerful magnetic currents, along the Earth's main meridian lines, which circle the entire globe dividing it into four quarters. It goes on to say that a "magnetic" island lies just north of the Streto de Anian (Bering Straits). (37)

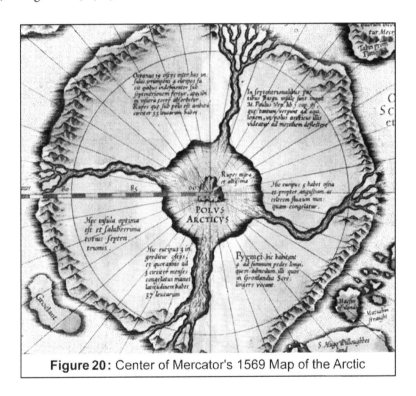

Figure 20: Center of Mercator's 1569 Map of the Arctic

On one of the large islands featured in the center of this Arctic map, it is clearly written in the legend:

"Pygmae hic habitant 4 ad summum pedes longi, quaemadmodum illi quos in Gronlandia Screlingers vocant."

"Translation: Here live Pygmies, at most 4 feet tall, who are like those called Scraelings in Greenland."

Who were these people that are mentioned with a supposed height of merely 4 feet, and where did they come from? The Carta marina (Latin "map of the sea" or "sea map"), was created in Rome and drawn by Swedish ecclesiastic Olaus Magnus in 1527-39. It is one of the first popular maps showing the Nordic countries in fine detail including place names. The Latin notes were translated by Olaus into Italian in 1565, and German in 1567. Olaus Magnus described the Pygmies of Greenland as small in stature, but big of heart.

Figure 21: European and Pygmy fighting on Greenland. Detail from the Carta Marina map, by Olaus Magnus

"Scraeling" is the Norse word for the various natives of the Arctic and the New World, including the mainland native Indians, the Dorset people of the islands, and the Eskimos who replaced the Dorsets in the early Second Millennium.(41) The word "pygmy" derives from the Greek word for a unit of measurement called "cubit". The Pygmies of antiquity were believed to be about a cubit or two high (18-36 inches). Pliny the Elder tells us that:

"Beyond these in the most outlying mountain region we are told of the Three-span men and Pygmies, who do not exceed three spans, i.e. twenty-seven inches, in height; the climate is healthy and always spring-like, as it is protected on the north by a range of mountains; this tribe Homer has also recorded as being beset by cranes. It is reported that in springtime their entire band, mounted on the backs of rams and she-goats and armed with arrows, goes in a body down to the sea and eats the cranes' eggs and chickens, and that this outing occupies three months; and that otherwise they could not protect themselves against the flocks of cranes that would grow up; and that their houses are made of mud and feathers and egg-shells. Aristotle says that the Pygmies live in caves, but in the rest of his statement about them he agrees with the other authorities" (Pliny the Elder, Natural History 7:23-30)

Battle of Pygmies and Cranes. (Pompeian Caricature.)

Figure 22: From Harpers Dictionary of Classical Antiquities

Homer's Iliad (760-710 B.C.) mentions the terrible and violent war between the large deadly cranes, and the valiant and courageous Pygmies. He compares the bloody battles of the Greeks and Trojans to the ferocity of the tireless battles between Pygmy and crane. (Homer, The Iliad, Bk 3:5)

Figure 23: Scene depicting of the battle between the Pygmies and the cranes, from the Francois vase (570 BC) found in 1844 in an Etruscan tomb, now displayed in the Museum of Florence

Pliny the Elder (23-79 A.D.) noted that the Pygmies were believed to have been displaced from their ancestral homeland by the crane's unrelenting onslaught. (Pliny the Elder, Natural History 4:44). He locates a remaining population of Pygmies somewhere mainly between Egypt and Ethiopia, though also having found a refuge as far afield as the Southeast of the North American continent.

Figure 24: Cranes v Pygmies Villa Silene, Leptis Magna, AD 6th

The Cherokees, whose ancestral home was in the southeast of North America, have a legend which tells of a journey by some men, who traveled south until they came upon a tribe of very little people, the Tsundige'wi, who barely reached up to a man's knee, and had strangely shaped bodies.(42) These little men and women lived in nests in the sand, that were covered with dry grass, and they were terrified of the wild geese, which came in great flocks from the south and attacked them.(43)

Figure 25: With the bravery of giants, the Pygmy people had to defend their shrinking territoty from larger invaders. Occasionally they had to fight against flocks of cranes and in these instances they would ride into battle on she-goats.

When the Cherokees arrived, the Tsundige'wi were in a state of great fear and anxiety, because the wind was blowing from the south, bringing with it some white feathers.(42) This was a sure sign that the birds were not for away. The Cherokees showed them new ways to defend themselves and how to use sticks and clubs so that they could hit the birds on their necks and kill them.(43)

Figure 26: Ancient Etruscan vase painting, 4th century B.C., depicting the battle between a Pygmy against a large crane.

As the birds flew in from the south in great flocks, the little men ran to their nests to hide. But when the birds stuck their long beaks into the nests and began to pull out the men out to eat them, the men dashed out with their clubs and hit the birds as the Cherokees had shown. They killed so many that after a while the birds flew away.(43)

Figure 27: Pygmy battle from the Nurenburg Chronicle 1493

For some time, the Tsundige'wi were able to keep the birds at bay, until eventually a flock of giant cranes arrived. These birds were much taller, and the little people weren't able to strike them on their necks, and so unfortunately for the Tsundige'wi, they all perished. (43)

Arab scholars agree with the fourteenth century Italian missionary and explorer Friar Odoric about tales told in China concerning remnant populations of Pygmaei struggling to survive against the continued predations of angry cranes in the Himalayas.(44) Chinese annals record similar accounts. The 5th Century Chinese religious text, the Shih King, states:

"In the region of Sihai is the land of the cranes where men and women are only seven inches tall. The only creatures they fear are cranes which come here from the sea. The cranes which in one single flight travel a thousand miles can gobble them up."(45)

According to the most ancient records from the Chinese, Scandinavians, Greeks, Romans, Arabs, and the Cherokee, we have an undeniable collective memory of an ancient, millennium long, and world-wide Pygmy vs. Crane war, resulting in victory for the crane and the near total extinction of the Pygmy. According to Homer:

"The cranes escape the winter time and the rains unceasing and clamorously wing their way to streaming Okeanos, bringing the Pygmaioi men bloodshed and destruction." - Homer, Iliad

Figure 28: Etruscan Vases, 4th Century B.C. depicting Pygmies battling cranes. State Hermitage Museum, St Petersburg, Russia

The ancient Greek grammarian, Antoninus Liberalis (around 100 A.D.), suggested that the Greek gods engineered this conflict as punishment against an immodest, and inadequately respectful queen of the Pygmies.(46) The Greek gods were known to have a nasty predilection for dealing out punishments far out of proportion to the seriousness of a given offense.

Figure 29: Pygmy fighting against a giant bird, Capital column, Autun Cathedral, Saone-et-Loire department, Burgundy, France

The Pygmies were eventually fractured, reduced to refugee status, and forced into exile.(46) Small clusters of them settled in Egypt, Ethiopia, Arctic Canada, and the Himalayas in an attempt to flee from the unstoppable cranes, who seemed determined to pursue them to the ends of the earth. Aristotle noted the presence of the giant cranes in Scythia,(47) as well as their continued destructive raids of Pygmaei refugee settlements south of Egypt:

"The cranes do this, for they travel from Scythia to the marshes in the higher parts of Egypt, from which the Nile originates. This is the place where the Pygmies dwell; and this is no fable, for there is really, as it is said, a race of dwarfs, both men and horses, which lead the life of troglodytes."(47)

Figure 30-a: A Pygmy fights a crane, Attic red-figure chous, 430–420 B.C., National Archaeological Museum of Spain

An October 2005 article, published by *The Circle of Ancient Iranian Studies*, reported finding the mummified remains of a person of small stature in Iran, which they believed were part of a "city of dwarfs ".(48) The article continued:

◇×

"Two months ago the illegal excavations in the historical fortress of Gudiz in Kerman province near Shahdad city, which dates back to the Sassanid era, led to the discovery of a 25-centimeter corpse known as the mummified dwarf which has brought a lot of questions to archaeologists.

"The corpse is covered by a thin layer, but experts believe that it must be a thin skin layer, and not materials used for mummification. A group of anthropologists will go to Kerman province in near future to determine the age and the gender of this corpse.

"The forensic medicine studies indicate that the corpse has remained quiet intact during excavations. It is estimated that the corpse must have been 16-17 years old at the time of death and is 20 to 25 centimeters high. The theory of the existence of a dwarf city in Kerman province was proposed by the discovery of this dwarf corpse, and the short height of the remained walls discovered in the area, but archaeological studies denies the existence of such a city in the province.

"Since forensic studies could not determine the sexuality of the corpse, we can not rely on them to talk about the height and the age of the body, and more anthropological studies are still needed to find out the details about the discovery," says Javadi, archeologist of the Cultural Heritage and Tourism Organization of Kerman province. "Even if it is proved that the corpse belongs to a dwarf, we can not say for sure that the region of its discovery in Kerman province was the city of dwarfs. This is a very old region, which has been buried due to geographical changes. Besides technology was not so developed at that time so people may not have been able to build high walls for their houses," he adds.

"Regarding the fact that in none of the periods in the history of Iran, we have had mummies, it is not accepted at all that this corpse is mummified. If this corpse is found to belong to Iran, it would be a fake one. Due to the minerals existing in the soil of this region, all of the skeletons here are decayed and no intact skeleton has been found so far. On the other hand the 38-year archeological excavations in Shahdad city deny any dwarf city in the region.

"The remained houses which their walls are 80 centimeters high were originally 190 centimeters. Some of the remained walls are 5 centimeters high, therefore should we claim that the people who live in these houses were 5 centimeters tall?" says Mirabedin Kaboli, head of archaeological excavations in Shahdad city.

"The 25 centimeter boy has been discovered in an Islamic cemetery. No inscription has been found indicating the date of the burial. The grave has been completely destroyed due to excavations, therefore the burial method is not clear at all."(48)

Figure 30-b: Kerman province near Shahdad city, Iran

In 2003, archeologists discovered a nearly complete skeleton of a tiny woman who lived about 17,000 years ago on the Indonesian island of Flores.(49) The skeleton's small stature (3'6") and reduced cranial capacity (400 cc, about a third the size of ours) caused anthropologists to assign this specimen to a new species, Homo floresiensis (famously known as the "Hobbit" by media), named after the island where it was discovered.(49)

Since the initial find, some teeth and bones belonging to as many as twelve H. floresiensis individuals have been found at the Liang Bua site, the bulk dated between 90,000 and 12,000 years ago. (49)

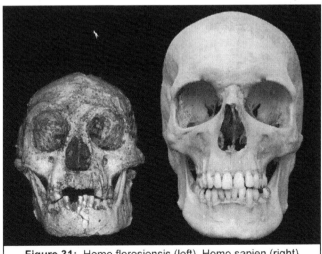

Figure 31: Homo floresiensis (left), Homo sapien (right)

In a 2010 article for *Live Science,* called "Giant Storks May Have Fed On Real Hobbits", Charles Choi describes fossils of giant storks, found in South East Asia, which could provide empirical evidence supporting the ancient "myth" of the Pigmy battles:

"The fossil remains of what may have been a hobbit-like species of human were discovered in 2003 at the Liang Bua cave on the Indonesian island of Flores. In that cave, scientists also unearthed a large number of bird fossils — including 20,000- to 50,000-year-old wing and leg bones from what appears to have been a stork nearly 6 feet tall (1.8 meters)."(50)

"Giant stork 'preyed on Flores hobbits'" was the headline on Britain's *Telegraph*, while *The Independent* went with, "Stork that ate babies, rather than delivering them" and the *Daily Mail* published, "Revealed: The giant stork that used to terrorize Indonesia's tiny 'hobbits.'" The Toronto Star asked "Were 'hobbit' humans killed off by giant storks?", implying that the disappearance of the unique Flores people was attributable to the 6 foot tall birds.(50)

The carnivorous giant (Leptoptilos robustus) was a hitherto unknown species of marabou stork recently discovered to have lived along side the "Hobbits" of Indonesia.(51) It was among the largest birds discovered standing at almost 6 feet tall, and they would have towered over the little people of Flores. Hanneke Meijer, a vertebrate paleontologist at the Smithsonian Institution in Washington, detailed the findings in the Zoological Journal of the Linnean Society:

"These birds are opportunistic carnivores — if you give them plenty of prey items, they'll hunt all of them. It was likely a ground-bound hunter, as its bones were thick, giving the bird an estimated weight of 35 pounds (16 kilograms). We're not certain as yet precisely why they all went extinct."(51)

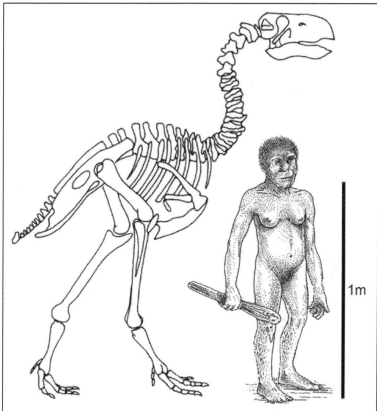

Figure 32: Artistic impression of the carnivorous giant stork (Leptoptilos robustus) next to a Hobbit (Homo floresiensis)

Hanneke Meijer and her colleagues now plan to investigate all of the bird fossils in the cave to figure out when species arrived or evolved and when they went extinct. This could give a better idea of what evolutionary forces were at work there, not only on the birds, but also the hobbits. "Stories like 'Lord of the Rings' do add a nice fantasy touch to my work," Meijer said.(51)

Research into Hominid DNA has recently confirmed that ancient humans 'rampantly interbred' during the Late Pleistocene (ice age) and indulged in interracial (cross-species) sex with multiple sub-races of different Hominid species.(52)

Figure 33: Artist depiction of different "races" of the Pleistocene

In September 2015, scientists announced the discovery of a previously unknown Homo species, called Homo naledi, found in a cave in South Africa, 50 km northwest of Johannesburg.(125) The remains of the ancient human-like species discovered last year have been analyzed by scientists who found that the ancient beings were dwarf-like and very similar to modern humans, despite being shorter and living some three million years ago.

With a brain the size of an apple, scientists claim the discovered skulls are marked similarity to our own and the species would have weighed under 100 pounds.(125) Perhaps the role of the stork, in the way early populations were introduced to each other, has been largely forgotten or filed away as "myth".

Figure 34: Sketch of giant stork carrying a Pygmy or "Hobbit"

Chapter 2

Antarctica is the last continent on earth with large, mysterious, unexplored areas that are still designated: "Terra Incognita", which means "Unknown Territory". It is estimated to be almost twice the size of Europe, and is mostly covered with a thick layer of ice. The thickness of this icecap varies, but in many places reaches several thousand feet. Scientists are still not certain as to its exact depths.

The Piri Reis map, a world map compiled in 1513 from much older documents, was drawn in Constantinople by the military intelligence of Admiral Piri Reis.(53) The original derived from documents dating back to at least the fourth century BC, and on information obtained by multiple explorers. It depicts various Atlantic islands, including the Azores and Canary Islands, as well as the mythical island of Antillia.

Figure 35: The Piri Reis map is a world map compiled in 1513 from military intelligence by the Ottoman cartographer Piri Reis

The Piri Reis map demonstrates the extent of exploration of the New World by the 1500's. It used ten Arab sources, four Indian maps sourced from the Portuguese, and one map of Columbus, famously featuring the controversial pre-modern exploration of the Antarctic coast.(53)

The map also depicts what is known as "Queen Maud Land," a one million square mile region of Antarctica as it looked during the Pleistocene (ice age). This region, and others shown in fine detail, are thought to have been covered completely in ice, but the map tells a different story. It shows this area as ice free, which suggests that these areas passed through a long ice-free period, a period which might not have come to an end until the current Holocene age.

According to the U.S. Air Force's cartographic department, in a reply letter to American professor Charles Hapgood:

"The claim that the lower part of the map portrays the Princess Martha Coast of Queen Maud Land, Antarctic, and the Palmer Peninsular, is reasonable. We have taken the old charts and the new charts that the Hydrographic Office produces today ⋯ we have found them to be in astounding agreement. The geographical detail shown in the lower part of the map agrees very remarkably with the results of the seismic profile made across the top of the ice-cap by the Swedish-British Antarctic Expedition of 1949."(53)

The USAF concluded— "This indicates the coastline had been mapped before it was covered by the ice-cap. The ice-cap in this region is now about a mile thick. We have no idea how the data on this map can be reconciled with the supposed state of geographical knowledge in 1513."(53)

This convinced Hapgood that the Piri Reis map showed the sub-glacial topography of Antarctica. The likely explanation for how this could be, he reasoned, was that it was mapped by a sophisticated lost civilization many thousands of years ago, before the ice sheet had formed over the continent. Hapgood published his thesis in his book *Maps of the Ancient Sea Kings* in 1966.(53) His research into ancient maps continued, however, as he states:

"I turned a page and sat transfixed. As my eyes fell upon the Southern Hemisphere of a world map drawn by Oronteus Finaeus in 1531, I had the instant conviction that I had found here a truly authentic map of the real Antarctica".(53)

Charles Hapgood was impressed because unlike the Piri Reis map, Oronteus Finaeus showed the entire Antarctic continent in fine detail, including minor rivers in the coastal portions of the landmass.

Figure 36: The Oronteus Finaeus map, published in 1531, shows Antarctica before it was "discovered" and free of ice

The world map of 1737 produced by French cartographer Philippe Buache, was also held in high esteem by Hapgood. It showed the entire continent of Antarctica, including the interior, as it appeared under the ice.(54) The modern world could not confirm it's accuracy until seismic surveys in 1958 mapped the whole sub-glacial topography of the continent.(55)

The Buache map depicts an ice free waterway dividing the continent into 2 landmasses. Although Antarctic is still today shown as one landmass, it is actually an archipelago of smaller islands separated by huge masses of ice. (54)

Buache claimed to have compiled his maps from much older sources, flirting with the possibility of some distant, lost, ancient sea-faring civilization with sophisticated map making skills.(54)

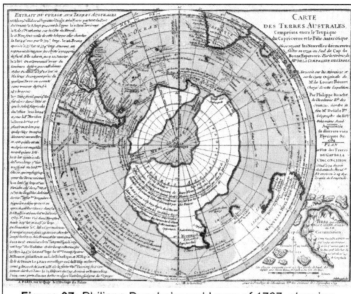

Figure 37: Philippe Buache's world map of 1737, showing Antarctic lands well before the continent was "discovered"

The first circumnavigation of Antarctica in recorded history took place in 1773 under the leadership of Captain James Cook.(56) In 1898, the German Imperial Valdivia Deep Sea Expedition left Hamburg on 31st July 1898 and returned on 1st May 1899. The ship had traveled over 32,000 nautical miles. The expedition was very successful. The results were published in 24 volumes, which took until 1940 to complete.(57) The next German expedition of 1926 charted the ocean floor in the area and discovered a 5,000 meter deep hole in the seabed.(57)

The Germans assembled a great store of information from these expeditions, and became the foremost firsthand authorities on Antarctica. Detailed maps were compiled and bodies of water were charted above and below the surface.

More German polar expeditions continued, from 1939 to 1945, but detailed information about them is still largely classified. During Hitler's chancellorship, German expeditions commuted fourteen times between the Antarctic area and the continents of Africa and South America, creating meticulous records of ocean depth, currents, air and water temperatures, and ice characteristics.(57) The massive amount of data was tabulated, classified, indexed, analyzed and studied by every branch of the Nazi regime. Because of the value this information has in U-boat (submarine) warfare, this justification was used to shroud it in secrecy.

Through his Minister of Foreign Affairs, Joachim von Ribbentrop, Hitler gave notice to the world of Germany's interest in the polar regions, setting in motion the preparations for colonization. The World Powers of the day, who were busy with their own colonial conquests in warmer territories, met Hitler's intention with near silence. Perhaps these German expeditions were seen as some sort of Nordic Aryan romantic interest, and written off as nationalistic propaganda.

In retrospect, it ironically turns out that the Piltdown man skeleton, which the British museum claimed to be the "missing link" during the entire first half of the 20th century turned out to be a fraud (58), while the ancient mythology concerning antediluvian polar civilizations subscribed to by the Nazis is continually receiving considerable scientific validation.

The third German Antarctic Expedition (1938–1939) was led by Alfred Ritscher (1879–1963), a captain in the Kriegsmarine (German navy). Kapitaen Alfred Kothas was chosen to lead the research ship "Schwabenland", which was lent by the German company Lufthansa.(57) The special badge or emblem of the Antarctic Expedition of 1938-39 features the "Hakenkreuz" (Hooked Cross), or Swastika symbol, clearly revealing the influential and deep, symbolic alliance with the German occult societies.

Figure 38: The SS Schwabenland and badge of the expedition

It is called 'Swastika' in India, 'Hakenkreuz' in Germany, 'Fylfot' in England, 'Tetra Gammadion' in Greece, 'Wan' in China, and 'Manji' in Japan.(58) Thomas Wilson, former curator of the Department of Prehistoric Anthropology in the U.S. National Museum, wrote about the Swastika symbol:

"An Aryan symbol used by the Aryan peoples before their dispersion.. an explanation how, as a sacred symbol, the Swastika might have been carried to the different peoples and countries in which we now find it".(58)

Hitler wanted to penetrate the entrances to the subterranean world known in mythology as Agartha (Asgard). He sought a way to get into direct physical contact with the descendants of the underground "Supermen" who he believed were responsible for the Swastika symbol's ancient dissemination and diffusion into cultures around the world. Hitler allegedly wanted to build an outer "Agartha" or "Aryana" with the subterranean race, reunited with Germany. Making this a reality was likely a primary motivation behind these dangerous and expensive voyages.

Figure 39: The 1938-1939 Third German Antarctic Expedition

The Book, *Secret Nazi Polar Expeditions*, articulates some of the scientific successes achieved and information gained from these German expeditions to Antarctica:

〰〰〰〰〰〰〰〰〰〰〰〰〰〰〰〰〰〰〰〰〰〰〰〰〰〰〰〰〰〰〰〰〰

"A sensational find was this region of warm-water lakes, all warm enough to swim in without special clothing, in fact, the men could swim in nothing at all! Moreover, the water was sweet and good to drink. The discovery of the warm water lakes in the Antarctic ice desert was like finding an oasis in the Sahara. Though surrounded by eternal ice and constant below zero temperature, the waters were heated—from below."(59)

〰〰〰〰〰〰〰〰〰〰〰〰〰〰〰〰〰〰〰〰〰〰〰〰〰〰〰〰〰〰〰〰〰

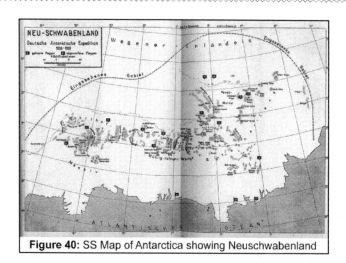

Figure 40: SS Map of Antarctica showing Neuschwabenland

Indeed, warm fresh water lakes are not what come to mind when one thinks of the frozen wasteland described by conventional scientists in the 1930's. This likely meant that there were volcanic vents providing thermal heat and possibly an active life cycle in the water beneath the ice.

One vast ice cave within the glacier extended 30 miles, to the large hot-water geothermal lake below the ice. Deep underground construction teams were dispatched on cargo ships, military transport ships, and U-boat. The ships from South Africa were protected by a host of U-boats and military ships. It goes on to say:

"The deep sub-sea trench discovered by previous German expeditions. Found to be of volcanic origin, it was discovered to run right through the new German colony of Neu-Schwaben-land, revealing itself in the form of warm water lakes, caves, crevasses and ice tunnels, most of which were found suitable for human habitation with the simple addition of electric lighting. The trench is an excellent deep sea route for U-boats."

Figure 41: German U-boat (Submarine)

A 2014 paper in *Nature Geoscience*, describes how gigantic tunnels as tall as the Eiffel Tower, have recently been discovered under the massive Antarctic ice sheets. The 820-foot tall tunnels, detected on airborne radar imaging and satellite photos, suggest that water flows in concentrated rivers in defined channels beneath the ice sheets. Scientists previously believed that melted water flowed beneath the ice sheets in more evenly-spread, thin, continuous sheets.

Geologists have also found an enormous 621 mile (1,000km) long canyon hidden underneath the Antarctic ice sheet. Research published in the journal *Geology* indicates that this mega chasm is 'bigger than the UK,' and is located in Princess Elizabeth Land, named in 1931 after Queen Elizabeth II. Around half a mile (1km) deep in places, the canyon is believed to have been carved out by water, but it is not known whether it was formed before or after the ice sheet grew.

The previous record for the longest known canyon, which was also discovered below the ice, was in 2013, but that one was located in Greenland and is a mere 460miles (750km) long. These canyons dwarf the Grand Canyon in Arizona, which, while a similar depth, is only 277 miles (445 km).

The newly discovered Antarctic canyon still has no official name. It was initially discovered by an examination of satellite imagery, followed by radio echo-sounding on sections the canyon. Radio-echo sounding (RES), also known as radio-glaciology, is the study of glaciers and ice sheets using radar. It uses electromagnetic radiation in the microwave band of frequencies on the radio spectrum to detect structures beneath the surface. Geologists also believe the canyon may be connected to another previously undiscovered, vast sub-glacial lake.

Edward Bulwer-Lytton authored *Vril: The Coming Race*, where he described a "superior" or advanced race, the Vril-ya, who lived in deep caverns beneath the earth and planned to conquer the world with a psychokinetic energy/force called Vril. The French author, Louis Jacolliot, furthered this idea in *Les Fils de Dieu* (*The Sons of God*) and *Les Traditions indo-européeenes* (*The Indo-European Traditions*). In these books, he linked vril with the legendary people of Thule, who also harnessed and exploited the power of vril to become Übermensch (Supermen) and rule the world. Most people considered these books works of fiction, but this did not include members of secret societies, such as those which developed into the National socialist party in Germany, who considered these stories at least partially based in truth.

The German Expedition to Tibet in the late 30's was at the invitation of the Tibetan Government. Nazi occult beliefs were not restricted to the mythical surface islands of Hyperborea, Thule or Atlantis, but extended to any vast inhabited "hollow" region inside of the Earth. The people of Tibet and Mongolia have always claimed that a cavernous underworld lies beneath the land. These Buddhist legends of tunnels leading to Shambhala were taken seriously by the local monks and surely contributed to the Nazi hope in contacting subterranean breakaway civilizations.

Maria Orsic was leader of the 'Vrilerinnen' or 'Vril Damen', the beautiful and allegedly psychic mediums of the German Vril Society. Dedicated to the study and practice of metaphysics and the occult, the sisters of the "Vril" conducted research into psychic phenomenon, time gravity manipulation, advanced propulsion technology, and saucer-shaped aircraft. (60)

Figure 42: Dedicated to the study and practice of metaphysics the maidens of Vril did not cut their hair, claiming that their long strands helped them facilitate contact with beings from beyond

Their secret society's members, including some who would later become high ranking leaders of the Nazi party, believed that many ancient civilizations owed their origins to refugees from places such as Atlantis, Hyperborea, Thule, Lemuria and others.(60) They zealously denounced the "out-of-Africa" theory as false science (see Piltdown man, Nebraska man, and other scientific falsifications) and as mere political propaganda.(58) The Vril society instead advanced the idea of subterranean civilizations ruled by an ancient parent-race that had mastered universal free-energy.

These breakaway civilizations, including the original Aryans that (re)established agricultural civilization during the Holocene, were said to have survived the antediluvian cataclysms which ended the Pleistocene,(58) and continued to thrive below the surface of the earth.

Following a major global catastrophe, as the Earth's surface stabilized and became slowly habitable again in the region of Mesopotamia, they emerged to form the dominant ruling nobility of the Sumerians and various other early societies.(58) They governed through an elite Aryan Rh-negative bloodline, and employed a segregated caste system; interracial cross-breeding (race mixing) was strictly taboo.(58,60)

After the German Antarctic Expedition explored it in 1938–1939, the Nazi party covertly proceeded to build massive subterranean bases deep under the Antarctic ice (see Base-211), continually shipping men and material to the South Pole throughout the war years.(59)

According to Russian researcher Konstantin Ivanenko:

"The Schwabenland sailed to Antarctica, commanded by Albert Richter, a veteran of cold-weather operations. The Richter

expedition's scientists used their large Dornier seaplanes to explore the polar wastes, emulating Admiral Richard E. Byrd's efforts a decade earlier. The German scientists discovered ice-free lakes (heated by underground volcanic features) and were able to land on them. It is widely believed that the Schwabenland's expedition was aimed at scouting out a secret base of operations."

Ivanenko claimed that the Antarctic Reich is "becoming more and more popular" in the countries of eastern Europe. He even issued a warning about potential political cooperation with this renegade group, "In the May 10, 2003 issue of the Frankfurter Allgemeine, Polish journalist A. Stagjuk criticized Poland's decision to send troops to Iraq" to assist with the Allied occupation. "At the end," he said, "The next Polish government will sign a treaty with Antarctica and declare war on the USA.'"

The Vril Society was formally founded as the "All German Society for Metaphysics". Its stated goal was to explore the origins of the Aryan race, to seek contact with the "hidden masters" of Ultima Thule, a legendary Nordic homeland, and to practice meditation, tantric yoga, and other guarded techniques intended to strengthen individual mastery of the divine Vril force itself.(60)

What is vril? Vril has often been compared to Orgone. Orgone is the universal "Life force", the basic building block of all organic and inorganic matter, and closely associated with sexuality (the term itself shares a root with the word orgasm). Coined by Dr. Wilhelm Reich, Orgone was seen as a massless, omnipresent substance, similar to luminiferous ether, and called by the great mystics and philosophers; Chi, Qi, or Prana.(60)

The belief in the existence of subtler, etheric states of matter was shared by Helena P. Blavatsky, foundress of Theosophy.(60) She writes:

"Occult science recognizes seven cosmic elements – four entirely physical, and the fifth (ether) semi-material. These seven elements with their numberless sub-elements (far more numerous than those known to science) are simply conditional modifications and aspects of the ONE and only Element."(60)

Edward Bulwer-Lytton's book published in 1871, The Coming Race, described an advanced civilization that dwelt below the surface and this mysterious energy called "Vril".(60) Blavatsky's recurrent homage to Bulwer-Lytton, and the Vril force, has exerted a lasting influence on other esoteric authors and occult groups, especially in Germany.

The psychic mediums of the Vril Society, led by Maria Orsic, claimed to have received information from an advanced race, who either dwelt in in deep, subterranean caverns inside the Earth, or lived in the Aldebaran star system. A second medium was known only as Sigrun, a name etymologically related to Sigrune, a Valkyrie and one of Wotan's nine daughters in Norse legend.(60)

With Hitler in power in 1933, the Vril Society received official state backing for continued disc development programs aimed at anti-gravitical flight and alternative energies to make the Third Reich independent of scarce fuel: oil.(60)

Today about one hundred German submarines remain unaccounted for, some equipped with the Walther Schnorchel (Snorkel), a device that allowed them to stay submerged for several weeks at a time.(59) If the secret Base-211 actually exists in Antarctica, it can be safely assumed that many Nazis fled to their under-ice refuge in Neuschwabenland with the dismantled Vril craft and their most advanced secret construction plans.(60)

In 1943, German Navy Grand Admiral Karl Dönitz stated:

"The German submarine fleet is proud of having built for the Führer in another part of the world a Shangri-La on land, an impregnable fortress."(60)

While it is widely accepted that the Nazis were defeated with the German Government's formal surrender in 1945, this is only partly true. Outpaced by the industrial war machine of the Allies, the Nazis gave up Germany in order to halt the perpetual carpet bombing of it's civilian population. There are persisting rumors that Germany had developed the atomic bomb before the Allies, but Hitler refused to use the weapon of mass destruction against entire Aryan populations. Instead, backdoor deals were struck allowing an exchange of technology, for the safe escape of hundreds of thousands of Nazis into South America, or employment in NASA and the CIA (see Operation Paperclip). The Nazi elite that escaped may have taken refuge in their Antarctic fortress.(60)

"The German submarine fleet is proud of having built for the Führer in another part of the world a Shangri-La on land, an impregnable fortress..."

- Karl Dönitz (1943)
German Navy Grand Admiral
Last President of a United Germany

Figure 43: German Navy Admiral Karl Dönitz (Left) and Chancellor/Führer of Nazi Germany Adolf Hitler (Right)

Hitler's body was never recovered,(61) and no Nazi party member ever signed any documents of surrender. That is why, after the Allies claimed unconditional victory, Secretary of Defense James Forrestal sent a naval task force, called "Operation Highjump," to Antarctica, including Admiral Nimitz, Admiral Krusen and Admiral Byrd.(62) Over 4,700 military troops from the U.S., Britain and Australia, consisting of three Naval battle groups departed on December 2, 1946.

With Admiral Byrd's command ship, the ice-breaker "Northwind," taking the lead, his convoy consisted of the catapult ship "Pine Island," the destroyer "Brownsen," the aircraft-carrier "Philippines Sea," the U.S. submarine "Sennet," two support vessels "Yankee" and "Merrick," and two tankers "Canisted" and "Capacan," the destroyer "Henderson" and a floatplane ship "Currituck."(62)

The US military and intelligence were apparently trying to locate the immense underground facility constructed by the Germans, before, during and immediately after the Second World War. The base was likely used to further their research and successful development of advanced propulsion technology and saucer-shaped aircraft, based on universal free energy.

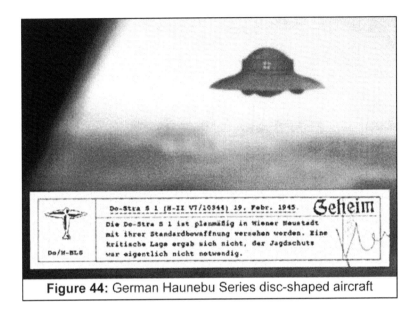

Figure 44: German Haunebu Series disc-shaped aircraft

According to first hand testimonials from crew members participating in Operation Highjump, including an interview given by Admiral Byrd himself, the Antarctic Nazis developed their saucer-shaped discs far in advance of anything possessed by the U.S.(63) They swiftly defeated the massive "post WW2" military attack by Allied forces.

The Allied invasion retreated in fear and disgrace, after suffering substantial damage and heavy casualties. Admiral Byrd was quoted in a newspaper article, which has been translated from the original in Spanish, during his first interview following this defeat.(63)

The March 5, 1947 edition of the Chilean newspaper *El Mercurio* carried the article from its correspondent, Lee van Atta, aboard the support ship Mount Olympus.(63) The title of the article was, "Admiral Richard E Byrd refers to the Strategic Importance of the Poles", and said:

"Admiral Richard E Byrd warned today of the need for the United States to adopt protective measures against the possibility of invasion

of the country by hostile aircraft proceeding from the polar regions. 'I don't want to scare anybody but the bitter reality is that in the event of a new war the United States will be attacked by aircraft flying in from the poles."(63)

Figure 45: Postage commemorating Admiral Byrd's expeditions

The media is largely controlled by the Rothschild banking dynasty,(64) and has promoted a false narrative concerning the events of WW2 for the past 70 years. While the United States government continues to suppress this "Vril" free-energy technology, maintaining the status quo of our oil-based globalist slave economy, the breakaway civilization created by the renegade Nazis are rumored to have established and successfully expanded an enormous secret space program which neither uses nor needs fossil fuels (oil).(65)

Top Secret maps obtained by the KGB and belonging to the Third Reich have been leaked on the internet which allegedly depict passages under the Antarctic ice used by German U-Boats to access mysterious underground polar caverns. However convincing, their authenticity still remains to be determined.

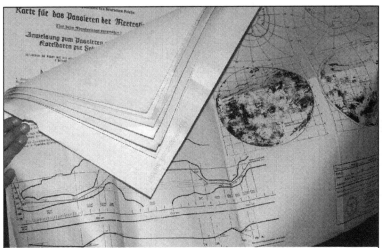

Figure 46: Documents allegedly belonging to the SS, which show U-boat routes beneath the Antarctic ice to inner Earth

That said, the possibility that the earth contains massive subterranean caverns, or is at least partially hollow, that these regions are accessible through passages at the poles, and that ancient secret breakaway civilizations flourish within them, has renewed people's interest in a subject still considered by the media to be taboo. Could the Earth really have entire inhabited cities underground that we are unaware of on the surface?

One of the most famous Hollow Earth proponents was John Symmes. He actively disseminated his "theory of concentric spheres and polar voids" until he died in 1829.(66) In a pamphlet,(67) Symmes candidly wrote:

"I declare that the Earth is hollow and habitable within; containing a number of solid concentric spheres, one within the other, and that it is open at the poles 12 or 16 degrees. I am ready to explore the hollow."(67)

He pledged his life to promoting his notion, and toured the US with a handmade wooden globe that opened out to reveal its secret internal layers. People were receptive to his ideas and his following grew.

Figure 47: Globe modified by Symmes to illustrate hollow Earth

His supporters began petitioning the government to finance his efforts to explore the earth's interior. On March 7, 1822 Senator Richard Thompson presented a case to Congress for Symmes to be supplied with "the equipment of two vessels of 250 to 300 tons for the expedition, and the granting of such other aid as Government may deem requisite".(66,68)

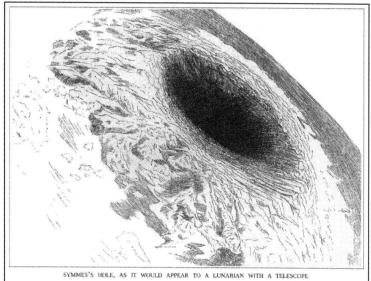

SYMMES'S HOLE, AS IT WOULD APPEAR TO A LUNARIAN WITH A TELESCOPE.

Figure 48-a: From Harper's New Monthly Magazine, 1882.

During the debate, it was suggested that the Committee for Foreign Relations become involved, as the trip may well bring Symmes and his crew into contact with new races of interior people. But the motion failed. Seven further bills were presented to the House, but not one of them succeeded.(66,68)

Symmes spent the rest of his life lecturing and lobbying for action. In May 1829, Symmes died, totally convinced, up until the end, that the greatest discovery in the history of mankind had eluded his grasp.

William Richard Bradshaw (1851–1927) was an Irish-born American author, editor, and lecturer who is known best for his novel, *The Goddess of Atvatabar*. His novel used Symmesian geography, from the ideas of John Symmes, to describe a utopian civilization living inside the Earth. In the story, a war breaks out among the people of Atvatabar when the subterranean Goddess falls in love with a man from the surface world. Following the conflict, contact is established with the surface world and trade relations are opened. It was published in 1892 and featured an illustration of the inner Earth.(126)

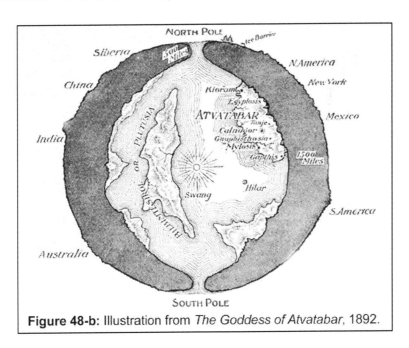

Figure 48-b: Illustration from *The Goddess of Atvatabar*, 1892.

Chapter 3

In *Man: Grand Symbol of the Mysteries: Thoughts In Occult Anatomy*, Honorary 33rd degree Freemason Manly P. Hall states:

"The most secret rituals of ancient initiation were performed in subterranean crypts, which were called 'caverns of the Mysteries.' In the Gothic rites, the final ceremony in which the new initiate was invested with the insignia of his order took place in a high, vaulted, cavernous chamber in the presence of the luminous statue of Balder... Here also are the Seven Sleepers of Ephesus and the cave-dwelling Rishis of India - the seven original beings who in the mythology of Central America were the cave-born progenitors of the races."(144)

In his book *The Chronicle of Akakor*, Karl Brugger gives the history of the Ugha Mongulala people, as provided to the author by the leader of their tribe. According to their chief, the tribe's ancestors were allegedly part of a vast empire which spanned across all of South America in ancient times.(140)

Some of their forefathers, the chief claimed, created vast subterranean cities beneath the Andes mountains and in parts of western Brazil.

In 1971, due to the constant encroachment of foreign settlers into their territory, 30,000 survivors of the Ugha Mongulala tribe allegedly escaped, seeking refuge inside the ancient network of underground cities. This inner earth kingdom allegedly consists of thirteen separate underground complexes, all connected by tunnels, with one extending all the way to Lima. Others are said to be located throughout the Andes Mountain range of Peru, as well as parts of Brazil.(140)

Mato Grosso (Portuguese for "Thick Bushes") is the third largest state in Brazil by area. It is known for a network of subterranean tunnels, and for being home to an ancient pre-Colombian light-skinned civilization associated with those tunnels.(69) Archaeologist Harold Wilkins remarks in *Mysteries of Ancient South America*:

"It is probable that descendants of this white empire exist, today, in more than one part of unexplored Brazil, and among the Andean outliers, in regions rich with gold, on the confines of the Amazon's headwaters. There are many stories of the existence of strange white people today - handsome bearded men and beautiful, white nude women with symmetrical Greek features - in the unknown sertao of the central Mato Grosso and the Brazilian highlands, and northwards and northwestwards in the mountains beyond the headwaters of the Amazon and its tributaries."(69)

In the Popol Vuh, an ancient Guatemalan manuscript whose title means 'The Collection of Written Leaves', and which has been described as the great storehouse of Mayan and Central American legend and mythical history, there is much talk of 'a land in the east on the shores of the sea'.(69) This description neatly fits Plato's position of Atlantis.

The Popol Vuh proclaims that it was from this land 'that the fathers of the people had come' and that they had also endured a 'great catastrophe' after which the land to the east disappeared.(69) Wilkins draws the ties between Atlantis and South America:

"One of the South American colonies of Atlantis may, probably, have been the land called Brazil, and Brazil, indeed, was actually the ancient name of the land and borne thousands of years before the arrival at Rio de Janeiro of old Pedro Cabral, the Portuguese navigator. That occurred in AD 1500 and has given rise to the sheer legend that King Emanuel of Portugal named the land Brazil, because the dye-wood, brazil-wood (Biancaea sappan) was found there. As a matter of very curious fact, the name Brazil was known to the old Irish Kelts as Hy-Brazil."(69)

In *The Hollow Earth*, Dr Raymond Bernard, an American archaeologist who now lives and continues to work in Brazil, reveals that:

"Mysterious tunnels, an enigma to archaeologists, exist in great numbers under Brazil, where they open on the surface in various places. The most famous is in the Roncandor Mountains of northwest Mato Grosso, to where Colonel Fawcett was heading when last seen."(64)

Lt. Colonel Percival Harrison Fawcett was a British archaeologist and South American explorer. Along with his eldest son, Fawcett disappeared under unknown circumstances in 1925 during an expedition to find "Z" – his name for a lost city, which he and others believed to be El Dorado, in the uncharted jungles of Brazil.(70)

Figure 49: Artist's impression of the Lost City of Z, believed by Col. Percy Harrison Fawcett to be in Mato Grosso, Brazil

Fawcett left behind instructions that if the expedition did not return, no rescue expedition should be sent lest the rescuers suffer his fate. During the following decades, various groups mounted rescue expeditions, without results. An estimated 100 would-be-rescuers died on the countless expeditions sent to uncover Fawcett's fate.(70) According to Dr. Raymond Bernard:

"Many Brazilian students of the occult share with the wife of Colonel Fawcett the belief that he is still living with his son Jack as residents of a subterranean city whose entrance is through a tunnel in the Roncador Mountain range of northeast Mato Grosso where he was heading when last seen after leaving Cuiaba. The writer met in Cuiaba a native who claimed that his father was Fawcett's guide and who offered to take him to a certain opening leading to the Subterranean World in the region of Roncador, which would indicate that Fawcett's guide believed in the existence of subterranean cities and brought Fawcett to one, where he was held prisoner lest he reveal the secret of its whereabouts, which he might be forced to do on his return, whether he wished to or not."(70)

Dr Bernard believed that the lost city Fawcett sought was of Atlantean origin, but was actually situated below ground. He claimed that the Atlantean city for which he searched was not the ruins of a dead city on the surface, but a subterranean city with still living Atlanteans as its inhabitants.(70)

In his 1960 essay, "The Mysterious Tunnels and Subterranean Cities of South America", the American Naturalist Carl Huni said:

"The entrance to the caverns is guarded by the Bat Indians, who are a dark-skinned, undersized race of great physical strength. Their sense of smell is more developed than that of the best of bloodhounds. Even if they approve of you and let you enter the caverns, I am afraid you will be lost to the present world, because they guard the secret very carefully and may not let those who enter leave."(71)

The popular rumor is that the subterranean cities they inhabit descended from the Atlanteans, who had originally constructed them, but many of the details surrounding their origin seem to have been lost or forgotten. The name of the mountain range where these underground cities exist is Roncador, in northeast Matto Grosso. If you go in quest of these caverns, you take your life in your own hands. Like Fawcett, you may never be heard of again.

According to John B. Leith, in the book *Genesis for the New Age,* there is another Germany ("New Berlin") inside the hollow surface of our planet. This inner or New Germany grew from the first or outer surface Germany. The story begins in 1572 when 500 Germans from Sax-Coburg, including some Prussians and Bavarians, were hired as soldier-mercenaries by the King of Portugal (Sebastian I) to build a fort and man a garrison up the Amazon River, in a fight against the Spaniards.(72)

As they sailed the river they were fiercely attacked by the Native Indians, and forced to flee to the jungles where they came across a cave entrance, which the Natives fled from in fear. The new colonists made their homes in and by the cave, and eventually traveled further inward and downward into the cave's passages, ultimately leading to the Earth's inner subterranean habitat - which they reached in 1647.(72)

Along the way, they settled into various caverns, establishing six cities along a 3,000 mile route, and they fought off mysterious cavern "creatures" who were as fierce as the Amazon Indians. The massive populated caverns or underground cities were connected by a crude wooden track system. (72)

In 1647, upon entering the inner concave surface, the New Germans met the lost ancestors of the modern Germans. Called Bods, they were extremely advanced, both spiritually and technologically, and decided to take their outer earth cousins under their wing. They became known as the Six Kingdoms of Saxony.(72)

The Macushi (Portuguese: Macuxi) Indians are indigenous to the Amazon. Nomadic hunter-gatherers, they mostly move between Brazil, Guyana and Venezuela. According to their oldest legends, they descended from the Sun's children ("Children of the Sun"), and the protectors of the "Inner Earth."(73)

Figure 50-a: Image by George Huebner (1895) Manau, Brazil

Their legends speak of an entrance into Earth, which was to remain secret to outsiders.(74) They would enter the Earth, and travel for 2 weeks until they reached the interior. It is there, "at the other side of the world, in the inner Earth" where the Giants live, people who stand around 3-4 meters in height.(74)

Figure 50-b: Unusually tall man from an indigenous tribe with Orlando Villas Boas, the State of Mato Grosso in Brazil, 1965

According to the Macushi, their people were given the sacred task of guarding the entrance, to prevent strangers from entering the interior of the Earth. Macushi legends state that those who enter the mysterious cavern travel for three days, descending giant stairs, which measure around 33" each step.

After the third day, they leave behind their torches, and continue their journey deeper into the Earth, illuminated by lights already present in the tunnels. Down deeper, they cross the lava zone, skirting an abyss where the incandescent magma (called lava when above surface) is bubbling. This is a very dangerous passage, the apprentice must be accompanied by an experienced guide, because many brave men have lost their lives in these hot chasms.(74)

After 4 to 5 days, those inside the cave would lose weight and corporeal mass, allowing them to move much faster. According to the legends, they seem to lose their weight the deeper down they go, until they almost float above the ground. It seems as if the gravitational force has disappeared. If this part of the story is true, it could imply that the climax of the Earth's gravity is not the center core, as mainstream science has suggested, but rather in the middle of the crust, in the middle of the magma zone, some 250 km deep.(74)

On the fifth day of traveling down the subterranean tunnels, according to the legends, they would come upon massive caverns whose ceilings could not be seen. In one of those chambers, a "sun-like" object provides light. It appears as a large glowing orb, which supposedly has the power to rejuvenate the beings it illuminates. The air is sweet, fragrant, far from the surface pollution. In the words of Macushi ancestors, the earth core is a paradise, filled with incredible wonders.(74, 75)

Inside the Earth, there are places where fruit trees are able to grow. The Macushi say that fruits like cajúes, oaks, mangos, bananas and some lesser plants can be found 6-7 days into their journey. The further the Macushi people moved into the Earth, the larger the areas with vegetation got. But not all the areas are green and prosperous. They warn that some places are extremely dangerous and should be avoided.(75)

The Macushi oral traditions continues to say that after passing these giant chambers, having passed half of their journey, they need to move carefully since the mysterious "air" can cause people to fly or float around. They would then reach a place where the Giants lived.(74)

There, the Macushi explorers would eat the food of the giants, including apples the size of human heads, grapes the size of a human's fist, and delicious and giant fish that had been caught by the Giants and given to the Macushi as gifts. After stocking up with food offered by the giants, the explorers would return home, to the outer world, helped by the Giants of the inner world.(74)

The Macushi are said to be the guardians of the underworld, the protectors of the entrance to the inner Earth. Their legends describe a land, inside the land, which is filled with amazing treasures and beautiful gem stones.(74,75) Many consider this legend a myth, just another ancient fairy tale. But to the Macushi, their legends were as real as it gets, and they protected the entrance.

Then, European explorers came to the Amazon in search of riches, ventured into the caves, and never returned. There were five Europeans, two Spanish and three Englishmen, thirsty for the gold and gemstones found in large quantities there.

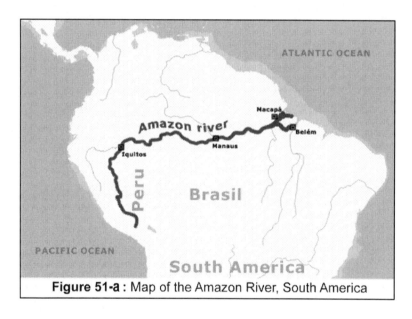

Figure 51-a : Map of the Amazon River, South America

Since then, the Macushi say that the Giants punished them for failing to fulfill their duties, and the legends of the Giants faded away with the years.(74) Is it possible that the Macushi legends are real, and somewhere in the Amazon, an entrance to the inner Earth existed in the past, or still does today?

In 2008, archaeologists in Mexico discovered eleven stone temples in underground caves, and an underground road that Mayans believe was the road to the mythical underworld city known as Xibalba.(145) According to ancient Mayan scripture, the Popol Vuh, the route to the underworld was filled with obstacles, including rivers filled with scorpions and blood, lined with houses shrouded in darkness or swarming with shrieking bats.(145)

Some of the newly discovered caves were submerged in water, and contained human bones, which the ancient Mayans believed was a portal, where dead souls entered the underworld. Excavations over the past five months in the Yucatan caves revealed stone carvings and pottery left for the dead.(145)

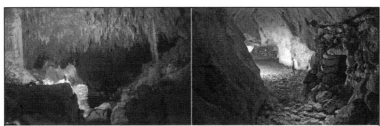

Figure 51-b: Archeologists Victoria Rojas and Lara Hindersten explore Mayan caves in Merida, Yucatan Peninsula, April 2008.

In Guatemala, archeologists have also discovered 800 km worth of tunnels which have been mapped underneath the Mayan pyramid complex at Tikal.

Figure 51-c: The Monumental Mayan architecture in Guatemala at Tikal dates back to the 4th century BC.

Tikal is an ancient Mayan citadel in the rainforests of northern Guatemala. Its iconic ruins feature the massive, ceremonial Lost World

Pyramid, the Temple of the Grand Jaguar. At 70 meters, Temple IV is the tallest pre-Columbian structure in the Americas. Could there be hidden passages built beneath the site? If so, who could have built them?

Patagonian giants are a legendary race of extremely tall people said to have inhabited the southern end of South America. They supposedly exceeded double the average height of a European man, some accounts giving heights from 8 or 9 feet, to over 14 feet tall.(76)

Figure 52: A map by Diego Gutiérrez from 1562, showing the "Gigantic Regio" (Region of Giants) and "Tierra de Patagones" (Land of Patagons)

The Giants were famously mentioned by Ferdinand Magellan and his crew, who claimed to have seen them while exploring the coastline of South America in the 1520s.(78) Antonio Pigafetta, a crew member and chronicler of Magellan's expedition, wrote about their encounter with natives twice a normal person's height:

<><><><><><><><><><><><><><><><><><><><><><><><><><><><><><><><><><><><><>

"One day we suddenly saw a naked man of giant stature on the shore of the port, dancing, singing, and throwing dust on his head. The captain-general [i.e., Magellan] sent one of our men to the giant so that he might perform the same actions as a sign of peace. Having done that, the man led the giant to an islet where the captain-general was waiting. When the giant was in the captain-general's and our presence he marveled greatly, and made signs with one finger raised

upward, believing that we had come from the sky. He was so tall that we reached only to his waist, and he was well proportioned. The captain named the people of this sort Pathagoni."(78)

Figure 53: Patagonian Giants - Dom Pernety, 1771

Many other accounts of giants in South America followed.(77,78) In 1579, Sir Francis Drake's ship chaplain, Francis Fletcher, wrote about encountering very tall Patagonian natives in *The World Encompassed*:

"Magellane was not altogether deceived, in naming them Giants; for they generally differ from the common sort of men, both in stature, bignes, and strength of body, as also in the hideousness of their voice."(77)

In the 1590s, Anthonie Knivet wrote that in Patagonia he had seen the bodies of dead Giants that were 12 feet (3.7 m) long.(78) Also in the 1590s, William Adams, an Englishman aboard a Dutch ship rounding Tierra del Fuego reported a hostile encounter between his ship's crew and abnormally tall and powerful natives. (76)

In 1766, Captain John Byron had circumnavigated the world in the HMS Dolphin. Word leaked that the crew had seen ten-foot tall giants in South America.(76) The official account of Byron's voyage, appearing in 1773, recounts:

"When we came within a little distance from the shore, we saw, as near as I can guess, about five hundred people, some on foot, but the greater part on horseback. . . . One of them, who afterwords appeared to be a Chief, came towards me: he was of a gigantic stature, and seemed to realize the tales of monsters in a human shape... these people may indeed more properly be called giants than tall men."

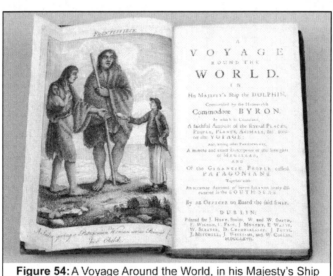

Figure 54: A Voyage Around the World, in his Majesty's Ship the Dolphin, Commanded by the Hon. Comm. Byron (1767)

Were the Patagonian Giants troglodytes? The Marble Caves of Patagonia, Chile, also called the Marble Cathedral, are considered by some to be the most beautiful cave network in the world. Formed by 6,000-plus years of waves washing up against calcium carbonate, the smooth, swirling blues of the cavern walls are a reflection of the lake's waters, which change in intensity and hue, depending on water levels and time of year.(79)

Figure 55-a: Marble Caves, Patagonia, Chile

In the year 2000, the "Cave of the Crystals" was discovered by miners excavating a tunnel for the Naica Mine in Mexico.(80) The main chamber contains some of the largest natural crystals ever found in any underground cave, with the cave's largest crystal found to date measuring at 36 feet (11 meters) in length, 13 feet (4 meters) in diameter and 55 tons in weight.

Figure 55-b: Mexico's Cave of Crystals connected to the Naica Mine 980 feet below the surface in Naica, Chihuahua, Mexico.

These spectacular crystals became so large because the extremely hot temperatures inside the cave, reaching a steamy 136 degrees Fahrenheit (58 degrees Celsius), encouraged microscopic crystals to form and rapidly grow.(80) Gazing at these gigantic crystals, one can't help but get carried away imagining what else awaits further exploration of these cave systems.

Figure 56: Giant Crystal Cave in Naica, Chihuahua, Mexico.

Chapter 4

The Hopi Indians maintain that their ancestors did not arrive from the north, nor by boat, but instead climbed onto the surface of the earth from the underworld.(81) The specific place of emergence of Hopi legend lies deep inside the Grand Canyon, an enchanted opening from the mysterious recesses of the earth.

The Native American lore associated with the Hopi, and some other tribes, states that the Grand Canyon was formed as a result of a Great Deluge, which had drowned the previous third world that had forgotten the path of divinity. They revere the Canyon as an "Eden", the beginning of the fourth, our present world.(81)

Hopi cosmology specifies that the Grand Canyon was the place of emergence from whence the Hopi emerged from their subterranean refuge after the flood had destroyed the third world.(81) Several inner world entry points are said to be located on Hopi land in the Canyon, one of which is honored in ceremony as the dwelling of an ancient god-like race.(82)

A dark opening in a rounded boulder, it is a place of pilgrimage for the Hopi, located at the bottom of the Canyon, by the Little Colorado River.(82) A sacred site, it is strictly off-limits to all but the Hopi people. The lore further claims that the Hopi were assisted by 'insect (ant) people' who lived in the inner world of caves and caverns, pale humanoids with thin limbs and slightly arched backs.(81,82)

Figure 57-a: Grand Canyon located in northwestern Arizona

The Hopi legends also speak of the Star People, who visited them. They considered themselves direct descendents from the Pleiades, who helped them as Gods. The Pleiadians are often said to have a Nordic appearance.(58)

The Smithsonian Institute may have discovered artifacts inside a massive cavern with intricate passages and rooms, including tablets bearing hieroglyphics, copper weapons, bronze tools, huge statues, which were described as appearing like Egyptian and Tibetan deities, as well as over 500 mummies (all male, assumed to be warriors). Most of these details are officially disputed. The explorer involved described a massive opening near the cave entrance, adorned with statues, somewhat like a cathedral.(83)

An article published in *The Arizona Gazette* on April 5, 1909, that the Grand Canyon was once home to a lost civilization, consisting of people of gigantic proportions. It also mentions the discovery of an enormous underground citadel by an explorer named G.E. Kinkaid, who came upon it while rafting on the Colorado River. (83)

Figure 57-b: The Arizona Gazette on April 5, 1909

This front page story detailed the exploration of a mysterious cave, which contained Egyptian hieroglyphics and Tibetan Buddhist-like statues. The entrance to the city was at the end of a tunnel that stretched for almost a mile underground.(83) Here is the text from the article:

Arizona Gazette, April 5, 1909

EXPLORATIONS IN GRAND CANYON

*Mysteries of Immense High
Cavern Being Brought
to Light*

"The latest news of the progress of the explorations of what is now regarded by scientists as not only the oldest archeological discovery in the United States, but one of the most valuable in the world, which was mentioned some time ago in the Gazette, was brought to the city yesterday by G.E. Kinkaid, the explorer who found the great underground citadel of the Grand Canyon during a trip from Green River, Wyoming, down the Colorado, in a wooden boat, to Yuma, several months ago.

"According to the story related to the Gazette by Mr. Kinkaid, the archeologists of the Smithsonian Institute, which is financing the expeditions,

have made discoveries which almost conclusively prove that the race which inhabited this mysterious cavern, hewn in solid rock by human hands, was of oriental origin, possibly from Egypt, tracing back to Ramses. If their theories are borne out by the translation of the tablets engraved with hieroglyphics, the mystery of the prehistoric peoples of North America, their ancient arts, who they were and whence they came, will be solved. Egypt and the Nile, and Arizona and the Colorado will be linked by a historical chain running back to ages which staggers the wildest fancy of the fictionist.

A Thorough Examination

"Under the direction of Prof. S. A. Jordan, the Smithsonian Institute is now prosecuting the most thorough explorations, which will be continued until the last link in the chain is forged. Nearly a mile underground, about 1480 feet below the surface, the long main passage has been delved into, to find another mammoth chamber from which radiates scores of passageways, like the spokes of a wheel.

"Several hundred rooms have been discovered, reached by passageways running from the main passage, one of them having been explored for 854 feet and another 634 feet. The recent finds include articles which have never been known as native to this country, and doubtless they had their origin in the orient. War weapons, copper instruments, sharp-edged and hard as steel, indicate the high state of civilization reached by these strange people. So interested have the scientists become that preparations are being made to equip the camp for extensive studies, and the force will be increased to thirty or forty persons.

Mr. Kinkaid's Report

"Mr. Kinkaid was the first white child born in Idaho and has been an explorer and hunter all his life, thirty years having been in the service of the Smithsonian Institute. Even briefly recounted, his history sounds fabulous, almost grotesque.

"First, I would impress that the cavern is nearly inaccessible. The entrance is 1,486 feet down the sheer canyon wall. It is located on government land and no visitor will be allowed there under penalty of trespass. The scientists wish to work unmolested, without fear of archeological discoveries being disturbed by curio or relic hunters.

"A trip there would be fruitless, and the visitor would be sent on his way. The story of how I found the cavern has been related, but in a paragraph: I was journeying down the Colorado river in a boat, alone, looking for mineral. Some forty-two miles up the river from the El Tovar Crystal canyon, I saw on the east wall, stains in the sedimentary formation about 2,000 feet above the river bed. There was no trail to this point, but I finally reached it with great difficulty.

"Above a shelf which hid it from view from the river, was the mouth of the cave. There are steps leading from this entrance some thirty yards to what was, at the time the cavern was inhabited, the level of the river. When I saw the chisel marks on the wall inside the entrance, I became interested, securing my gun and went in. During that trip I went back several hundred feet along the main passage till I came to the crypt in which I discovered the mummies. One of these I stood up and photographed by flashlight. I gathered a number of relics, which I carried down the Colorado to Yuma, from whence I shipped them to Washington with details of the discovery. Following this, the explorations were undertaken.

The Passages

"The main passageway is about 12 feet wide, narrowing to nine feet toward the farther end. About 57 feet from the entrance, the first side-passages branch off to the right and left, along which, on both sides, are a number of rooms about the size of ordinary living rooms of today, though some are 30 by 40 feet square. These are entered by oval-shaped doors and are ventilated by round air spaces through the walls into the passages. The walls are about three feet six inches in thickness.

"The passages are chiseled or hewn as straight as could be laid out by an engineer. The ceilings of many of the rooms converge to a center. The side-passages near the entrance run at a sharp angle from the main hall, but toward the rear they gradually reach a right angle in direction.

The Shrine

"Over a hundred feet from the entrance is the cross-hall, several hundred feet long, in which are found the idol, or image, of the people's god, sitting cross-legged, with a lotus flower or lily in each hand. The cast of the face is oriental,

and the carving this cavern. The idol almost resembles Buddha, though the scientists are not certain as to what religious worship it represents. Taking into consideration everything found thus far, it is possible that this worship most resembles the ancient people of Tibet.

"Surrounding this idol are smaller images, some very beautiful in form; others crooked-necked and distorted shapes, symbolical, probably, of good and evil. There are two large cactus with protruding arms, one on each side of the dais on which the god squats. All this is carved out of hard rock resembling marble. In the opposite corner of this cross-hall were found tools of all descriptions, made of copper. These people undoubtedly knew the lost art of hardening this metal, which has been sought by chemicals for centuries without result. On a bench running around the workroom was some charcoal and other material probably used in the process. There is also slag and stuff similar to matte, showing that these ancients smelted ores, but so far no trace of where or how this was done has been discovered, nor the origin of the ore.

"Among the other finds are vases or urns and cups of copper and gold, made very artistic in design. The pottery work includes enameled ware and glazed vessels. Another passageway leads to granaries such as are found in the oriental temples. They contain seeds of various kinds. One very large storehouse has not yet been entered, as it is twelve feet high and can be reached only from above. Two copper hooks extend on the edge, which indicates that some sort of ladder was attached. These granaries are rounded, as the materials of which they are constructed, I think, is a very hard cement. A gray metal is also found in this cavern, which puzzles the scientists, for its identity has not been established. It resembles platinum. Strewn promiscuously over the floor everywhere are what people call 'cats eyes,' a yellow stone of no great value. Each one is engraved with the head of the Malay type.

The Hieroglyphics

"On all the urns, or walls over doorways , and tablets of stone which were found by the image are the mysterious hieroglyphics, the key to which the Smithsonian Institute hopes yet to discover. The engraving on the tables probably has something to do with the religion of the people. Similar hieroglyphics have been found in southern Arizona. Among the pictorial writings, only two animals are found. One is of prehistoric type.

The Crypt

"*The tomb or crypt in which the mummies were found is one of the largest of the chambers, the walls slanting back at an angle of about 35 degrees. On these are tiers of mummies, each one occupying a separate hewn shelf. At the head of each is a small bench, on which is found copper cups and pieces of broken swords. Some of the mummies are covered with clay, and all are wrapped in a bark fabric.*

"*The urns or cups on the lower tiers are crude, while as the higher shelves are reached, the urns are finer in design, showing a later stage of civilization. It is worthy of note that all the mummies examined so far have proved to be male, no children or females being buried here. This leads to the belief that this exterior section was the warriors' barracks.*

"*Among the discoveries no bones of animals have been found, no skins, no clothing, no bedding. Many of the rooms are bare but for water vessels. One room, about 40 by 700 feet, was probably the main dining hall, for cooking utensils are found here. What these people lived on is a problem, though it is presumed that they came south in the winter and farmed in the valleys, going back north in the summer.*

"*Upwards of 50,000 people could have lived in the caverns comfortably. One theory is that the present Indian tribes found in Arizona are descendants of the serfs or slaves of the people which inhabited the cave. Undoubtedly a good many thousands of years before the Christian era, a people lived here which reached a high stage of civilization. The chronology of human history is full of gaps. Professor Jordan is much enthused over the discoveries and believes that the find will prove of incalculable value in archeological work.*

"*One thing I have not spoken of, may be of interest. There is one chamber of the passageway to which is not ventilated, and when we approached it a deadly, snaky smell struck us. Our light would not penetrate the gloom, and until stronger ones are available we will not know what the chamber contains. Some say snakes, but other boo-hoo this idea and think it may contain a deadly gas or chemicals used by the ancients. No sounds are heard, but it smells snaky just the same. The whole underground installation gives one of shaky nerves the creeps. The gloom is like a weight on one's shoulders, and our flashlights and candles only make the darkness blacker. Imagination can revel in conjectures and ungodly daydreams back through the ages that have elapsed till the mind reels dizzily in space."*

An Indian Legend

"In connection with this story, it is notable that among the Hopi Indians the tradition is told that their ancestors once lived in an underworld in the Grand Canyon till dissension arose between the good and the bad, the people of one heart and the people of two hearts. Machetto, who was their chief, counseled them to leave the underworld, but there was no way out. The chief then caused a tree to grow up and pierce the roof of the underworld, and then the people of one heart climbed out. They tarried by Paisisvai (Red River), which is the Colorado, and grew grain and corn.

"They sent out a message to the Temple of the Sun, asking the blessing of peace, good will and rain for people of one heart. That messenger never returned, but today at the Hopi villages at sundown can be seen the old men of the tribe out on the housetops gazing toward the sun, looking for the messenger. When he returns, their lands and ancient dwelling place will be restored to them. That is the tradition.

"Among the engravings of animals in the cave is seen the image of a heart over the spot where it is located. The legend was learned by W.E. Rollins, the artist, during a year spent with the Hopi Indians.

"There are two theories of the origin of the Egyptians. One is that they came from Asia; another that the racial cradle was in the upper Nile region. Heeren, an Egyptologist, believed in the Indian origin of the Egyptians. The discoveries in the Grand Canyon may throw further light on human evolution and prehistoric ages."(83)

Even before this article, the Arizona Gazette published a short piece pertaining to the Grand Canyon discoveries:

Arizona Gazette, March 12, 1909

G. E. KINCAID REACHES YUMA

"G. E. Kincaid of Lewiston, Idaho, arrived in Yuma after a trip from Green River, Wyoming, down the entire course of the Colorado River. He is the

second man to make this journey and came alone in a small skiff, stopping at his pleasure to investigate the surrounding country. He left Green River in October having a small covered boat with oars, and carrying a fine camera, with which he secured over 700 views of the river and canyons which were unsurpassed. Mr. Kincaid says one of the most interesting features of the trip was passing through the sluiceways at Laguna dam. He made this perilous passage with only the loss of an oar. Some interesting archaeological discoveries were unearthed and altogether the trip was of such interest that he will repeat it next winter in the company of friends." (84)

Another lesser known subterranean location, presumed to be familiar to the Native Americans, is right below Los Angeles, California.(85) Its discovery made front page news.

In 1933, a mining engineer named G. Warren Shufelt was surveying the L.A. area for oil, gold and other valuable materials. He discovered what appeared to be a well planned underground labyrinth, with large rooms located at various points, and deposits of apparently man made gold in the chambers and passage ways.(85)

Some of the tunnels ran west for 20 miles under the Santa Monica Bay. Shuffle believed these tunnels were only used for ventilation. He proceeded to draw a map and had it copyrighted.(85)

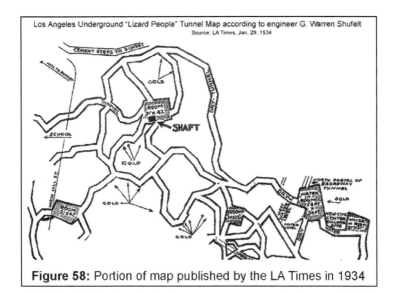

Figure 58: Portion of map published by the LA Times in 1934

A Hopi Indian named Chief Little Green Leaf told him about the legend of an ancient race of "Lizard People", explaining that around 4,000 years ago, fire from the sky fell on the western coast and covered an area hundreds of miles wide. Winslow crater in northern Arizona is only one of the pieces that rained down at that time. Thousands were killed, their crops wiped out, their homes destroyed, and the forests set ablaze. The survivors from a gigantic meteor shower, which devastated most of the western coastal US, found shelter underground.(85)

Shufelt and Chief Little Green Leaf were convinced that the ancient legends and the readings from Shufelt's mystery machine were true. They decided to obtain a permit to sink a shaft into the ruins of the subterranean city.(85) On 29th January 1934, the first story regarding the legend of the "Lost Land of the Lizard People" made the L.A. newspapers:

Los Angeles Times, January 29, 1934

Lizard People's Catacomb City Hunted

Engineer Sinks Shaft Under Fort Moore Hill to Find Maze of Tunnels and Priceless Treasures of Legendary Inhabitants

By: Jean Bosquet

"Busy Los Angeles, although little realizing it in the hustle and bustle of modern existence, stands above a lost city of catacombs filled with incalculable treasure and imperishable records of a race of humans further advanced intellectually than the highest type of present day peoples, in the belief of G. Warren Shufelt, geophysicist mining engineer now engaged in an attempt to wrest from the lost city deep in the earth below Fort Moore Hill the secrets of the Lizard People of legendary fame in the medicine lodges of the American Indian.

"So firmly does Shufelt and a little staff of assistants believe that a maze of catacombs and priceless golden tablets are to be found beneath downtown Los Angeles that the engineer and his aids have already driven a shaft 250 feet into the ground, the mouth of the shaft being on the old Banning property on North Hill street, overlooking Sunset Boulevard, Spring street and North Broadway.

"And so convinced is the engineer of the infallibility of a radio x-ray perfected by him for detecting the presence of minerals and tunnels below the surface of

the ground, an apparatus with which he says he has traced a pattern of catacombs and vaults forming the lost city, that he plans to continue sending his shaft downward until he has reached a depth of 1000 feet before discontinuing operations.

LEGEND SUPPLIES CLEW

"Shufelt learned of the legend of the Lizard People after his radio X-Ray had led him hither and yon, over an area extending from the Public Library on West Fifth street to the Southwest Museum, on Museum Drive, at the foot of Mt. Washington.

"I knew I was over a pattern of tunnels," the engineer explained yesterday, "and I had mapped out the course of the tunnels, the position of large rooms scattered along the tunnel route, as well as the position of deposits of gold, but I couldn't understand the meaning of it."

"Then Shufelt was taken to Little Chief Greenleaf of the medicine lodge of the Hopi Indians in Arizona, who's English name is L. Macklin. The Indian provided the engineer with a legend which, according to both men, dovetails exactly with what Shufelt say he has found.

FIRE DESTROYS ALL

"According to the legend as imparted to Shufelt by Macklin, the radio X-Ray has revealed the location of one of the three lost cities on the Pacific Coast, the local one having been dug by the Lizard People after the "great catastrophe" which occurred about 5000 years ago. This legendary catastrophe was in the form of a huge tongue of fire, which "came out of the Southwest, destroying all in it's path," (continued on Page 5, Column 2) "...the path being several hundred miles wide." The city underground was dug as a means of escaping future fires.

"The lost city, dug with powerful chemicals by the Lizard People instead of pick and shovel, was drained into the ocean, where it's tunnels began, according to the legend. The tide passing daily in and out of the lower tunnel portals and forcing air into the upper tunnels, providing ventilation and "cleansed and sanitized the lower tunnels," the legend states.

"Large rooms in the domes of the hills above the city of labyrinths housed 1000 families "in the manner of tall buildings" and imperishable food supplies of the herb variety were stored in the catacombs to provide sustenance for the Lizard folk for great length of time as the next fire swept over the earth.

CITY LAID OUT LIKE LIZARD

"The Lizard People, the legends has it, regard the lizard as a symbol of long life. Their city is laid out like a lizard, according to the legend, it's tail to the Southwest, far below Fifth and Hope streets, it's head to the northeast, at Lookout and Marda streets. The city's key room is situated directly under South Broadway, near Second street, according to Shufelt and the legend.

"This key room is the directory to all the parts of the city and to all record tablets, the legend states. All records were to be kept on golden tablets, four feet long and fourteen inches wide. One these tablets of gold, gold having been the symbol of life to the legendary Lizard People, will be found the record of history of the Mayans and on one particular tablet, the southwest corner of which will be missing, is found the "record of the origin of the human race."

TABLETS PHOTOGRAPHED

"Shufelt stated he has taken "X-Ray pictures" of thirty-seven such tablets, three of which have their southwest corners cut off.

"My radio X-ray pictures of the tunnels and rooms, which are subsurface voids, and of gold pictures with perfect corners, sides and ends, are scientific proof of their existence," Shufelt said. "However, the legendary story must remain speculative unearthed by excavation."

"The Lizard People, according to Macklin, were of a much higher type of intellectuality than modern human beings. the intellectual accomplishments of their 9-year-old children were of equal of those of present day college graduates, he said. So greatly advanced scientifically were these people that, in addition to perfecting a chemical solution by which they bored underground without removing any earth and rock, they also developed a cement far stronger and better than any in use in modern times which they lined their tunnels and rooms.

HILLS ENCLOSE CITY

"Macklin said legendary advise to American Indians was to seek the lost city in an area within a chain of hills forming "the frog of a horses hoof." The *contour of hills surrounding this region forms such a design, substantiating Shufelt's findings, he said.*

"Shufelt's radio device consists chiefly of a cylindrical glass case inside which a plummet attached to a copper wire held by the engineer sways continually, pointing he asserts, toward minerals or tunnels below the surface of the ground, and then revolves when over mineral or swings in prolongation of the tunnel when above the excavation. He has used the instrument extensively in mining fields, he said." (85)

Mr. Arche Dunning of the Los Angeles Chamber of Commerce stated in December of 1947 that:

"It is quite possible, of course, that the supposed labyrinth really exists. But in view of the fact that the overlaying area is the immediate Civic Center area where an important building program is to be carried out, including federal, state, county and city building, there is little probability of any further excavations."(85)

That was the last article that the *LA Times* published on any planned subterranean excavations of the tunnels below Los Angeles, but interest in the story has never gone away.

Located in central Kentucky and covering well over 52,000 acres, the Mammoth Cave was established as a national park in 1941, and as a World Heritage Site in 1981. With a staggering 400 miles (640 km) of surveyed passageways, Mammoth Cave is by far the world's longest known cave system, over twice as long as the second-longest cave system, Mexico's Sac

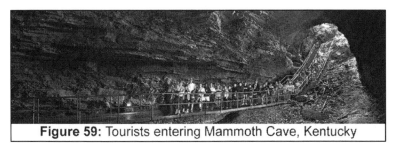

Figure 59: Tourists entering Mammoth Cave, Kentucky

Actun underwater cave. Archeologists are constantly making new discoveries and additional connections in this cave system, adding several miles to this figure each year. (86)

Although many woolly mammoth specimens have been discovered at the Big Bone Lick State Park in Kentucky, no fossils of the woolly mammoth have ever been found in Mammoth Cave. The name of the cave has nothing to do with this extinct mammal, but rather, the name "Mammoth" refers to the gigantic width and incredible length of the passages which connect to the Rotunda just inside the entrance.(86)

While surface animals may take refuge in the entrances of the caves, they do not generally venture into the deep. The following species of bats inhabit the caverns: Indiana bat (Myotis sodalis), gray bat (Myotis grisescens), little brown bat (Myotis lucifugus), big brown bat (Eptesicus fuscus), and the eastern pipistrelle bat (Pipistrellus subflavus). (87)

Other animals which inhabit the caves include: Two genera of crickets (Hadenoecus subterraneus) and (Ceuthophilus stygius) (Ceuthophilus latens), a cave salamander (Eurycea lucifuga), two genera of eyeless cave fish (Typhlichthys subterraneus) and (Amblyopsis spelaea), and a cave crayfish (Orconectes pellucidus). Mammoth Cave is also home to the endangered Kentucky cave shrimp (Palaemonias ganteri), a sightless albino shrimp.(87)

The Echo River Tour, one of the cave's most famous attractions, took visitors on a boat ride along an underground river, but the tour was discontinued in the early 1990sfor logistic and environmental reasons.

Figure 60: Echo River 360 Ft Underground Mammoth Cave, KY

Several sets of Native American remains have been recovered from Mammoth Cave. Many of these mummified remains indicate intentional pre-Columbian funerary practice.(87) Another fascinating discovery was the remains of cane torches used by Native Americans. Other artifacts such as drawings, gourd fragments, and woven grass moccasin slippers have been discovered deep inside the cavern system.(88)

Various federal and state laws protect the ancient human remains and artifacts within the caves. Explorers are properly trained not to disturb archaeological evidence, and some areas remain out-of-bounds even to seasoned explorers.

H.P. Lovecraft's short story, *The Beast in the Cave*, is set in Mammoth Cave.(89) He finished the final draft in 1905, when he was fourteen, and published it in the June 1918 issue of the amateur press journal, *The Vagrant*. The plot involves a man on a tour of Mammoth Cave who separates from his guide and becomes lost. His torch finally expires, leaving him hopeless of finding a way out in the pitch dark.(89)

He then hears strange sounding footsteps approaching. Thinking it a lost mountain lion, he desperately throws a stone at the source of the sound. The beast is hit and crumples to the floor. The guide eventually finds the protagonist, and together they examine the fallen creature with the guide's torchlight. As the creature mutters its last breaths, revealing its face, they discover that it is a pale, deformed human, who actually had lived in the caves for years.(89)

Figure 61: Carlsbad Caverns National Park - New Mexico

Carlsbad Caverns, a National Park located near Carlsbad, New Mexico., includes the "Big Room", a natural limestone cave chamber which measures 1,219 by 190 meters (4,000 by 625 feet), and 107 meters (350 feet) high at the highest point. It is the seventh largest cave chamber in the world.(135)

The Carsbad Caverns are decorated with stalactites, stalagmites, and an incredible variety of other formations, which can be seen along several easily accessible trails. These massive caverns might provide insight into what one might find at much deeper depths, down below the crust of the Earth.

In the October 1947 issue of *Amazing Stories*, there appears the following account:

◇◇

"Norman Finley, a neighbor of a good friend of mine, told me about an experience he had which was rather unusual. He and a couple of other fellows were hunting down in the Big Bend country. I don't know whether you are familiar with the Big Bend or not, but there is no more wild or desolate area in the country. Rugged, mountainous, cut by canyons, there are innumerable parts of it which have never known the foot of man.

"It was in one of the most desirable areas that Finley and his companions found themselves. They had driven about ninety miles southwest of Marathon, Texas, a little town of about 700 people, at the foot of the Del Norte Mountains, 4000 feet high, and had then gone on afoot. The dirt road just petered out and they couldn't get their car further. They were hunting deer but had no luck. Just as they were about to call it a day, Finley spotted a mountain lion. He snapped a shot at it and knocked it over. But the lion just rolled over on his feet and started to leave those parts.

"Finley and the other fellows took after him, since it was obvious that he was wounded and not making very good time. They managed to keep him in sight for about a mile and were sure they had him when he ran into a box canyon. The lion, however, started up a faint trail up one side of the canyon to a small cave they could see about a

hundred feet from the floor of the canyon. They followed him up this trail, but when they got to the cave - there was no lion!

"The cave was one of those dished-out affairs that are so common in the southwest. Eroded out of the face of a cliff and cup-shaped. The only access to it was by that trail. But this cave was a bit queer. It had a sand floor and was just about big enough to park twenty cars in it. On the cliff edge was a low STONE WALL. This in itself was not too unusual, because such caves have sheltered Indians for thousands of years.

"The thing that did make it unusual was that in the rear of it was a perfectly round hole. It was obvious that the lion had ducked into this.

"They approached it rather cautiously and tossed some stones in it to see if they could stir him up. But there was no response. They could hear the stones rolling and bouncing down an incline and the sound just got fainter and fainter until it died away altogether.

"They then approached the hole and peered down into it. It was perfectly round - also it was about four or five feet in diameter. They couldn't see very far down it, but it appeared to descend rather sharply and at a steady gradient. The fellows gathered some dry grass from the canyon floor and made some torches. The incline of the bore was too steep for them to climb down so they tossed the torches down it. They just slid down further and further and disappeared into the gloom. They never did see or hear of the lion again.

"At first they thought they had stumbled onto some old Spanish mine workings. But there was no sign anywhere of a dump that always goes with a mine. By all rights there should have been some sign of the earth and rock that had come out of that hole - but there wasn't.

"When they inspected the hole itself more closely, they were amazed at it's symmetry and at the consistency of the section of the bore as far as they could see down it. The fact that the bore was perfectly round puzzled them, too. If it was a mine shaft, it most certainly wouldn't have been round, but instead would have been flat on the *bottom. The fact that the shaft extended straight and unwavering as a rigid pipe was cause for further amazement. Since the fellows had no rope with them, which would have been needed to descend the shaft, as well as lights, they scratched their heads awhile and then left.*

"Finley wanted to go back with equipment and see how far down the shaft went and what was at the bottom of it. But ranchers are busy people and he never went back. In the meantime he got pretty well broken up when a horse threw him and he now lives in Fort Worth while he has someone else to run the ranch. We talked rather idly about having a look at his cave someday. He says he knows exactly where it is and could find that box canyon with his eyes shut. So far we haven't done anything about it. But we may either this summer or next when we get time to go down to Big Bend.

"Finley told me this story about a year before even you heard of Shaver so you can be sure he wasn't influenced by the 'Shaver Mystery.' In fact, I don't believe he has ever heard of the 'Shaver Mystery,' even to this day.

"E. Stanton Brown., 4931 Bryce Ave., Fort Worth 7, Texas."(134)

The following year, *Amazing Stories* published another letter concerning underground activity around Texas, confirming that strange phenomena may exist in the state's western part, but this time the strangeness extends to the border of New Mexico:

"The mysterious cave Mr. E. Stanton Brown spoke of in his letter is not exactly news to me. In 1938 a party of six of my friends and myself spent seven months in that area of Texas, and upper Mexico. We were testing an electronic instrument that we had developed, and needed lots of space and some mineral deposits for the various tests. So, we got rather well acquainted with the Big Bend country, and the Figure 2 Ranch north of there. We arrived there in January and camped IN THE SIERRA BLANCAS, storing a lot of our equipment

at the town of Van Horn. By March we had gotten deep into the rugged country and as I recall, it was about the middle of March we stumbled onto this cave (or a twin) that Mr. Brown speaks of in his letter. Everyone was so dumbfounded by it that we spent the better part of the rest of the month in making a thorough investigation. We penetrated the shaft to a distance of 870 feet and at about 650 feet found some very finely executed writing on the right wall at eye level, IN WHAT RESEMBLES CUNEIFORM. At 800 feet one of the party fell over a cloth lying in the dust, and upon closer examination, it was found to be part of a blue shirt, of fairly recent manufacture; indicating that someone else had been this far in recent times. This and an empty pint whiskey bottle dated 1897 was all we located to indicate recent occupation. Of course in a country where desperadoes such as Black Jack, Billy the Kid, etc., hid out where they could and the more solitary the better, such a find was not too surprising.

"At about 780 feet the floor dips more sharply downward and at near 900 feet progress is very hazardous due to moisture and increased slant downward. We carried rocks from the opening, and rolled them from the point where we could no longer walk, but they simply faded out with a rumble after a few seconds. We tried rolling flaming yucca stumps to see if, perhaps, we might determine more about the bore further on, but this proved to be futile, since the stumps burned poorly at best, probably due to bad air. It was very stuffy and hot after the first 300 feet from the opening. We held a powwow to try and figure out how we could go further down, but the only thing would have been lots of lariat ropes, or a long steel cable, and neither was available nearer than some 50 miles.

"If Mr. Finley had taken the time to go hunting up in the Figure 2 Ranch territory he might have run across another, and to me more interesting, cave than the Big Bend one. About 62 miles north from the town of Van Horn you go through the salt-flat country, where the Salt Wars of the old west occurred. Westward, some 8 or 9 miles from the road is the Apache Canyon country, and as rugged as anywhere on the face of the globe. In an offshoot of Apache Canyon to the south, is an almost impassable gash called Hell Canyon. The walls of *this canyon rise precipitously for at least 1000 feet and top out on Apache Peak on one side and an old Indian ceremonial ground on the other side. More desolate country would be hard to imagine. Coyotes and mountain lions are plentiful, and panthers no novelty. I have seen as many as 34 deer in a herd down below on the grassy ledge sloping down toward the canyon floor. Of course, further up toward the box end of the canyon it was much too rugged for deer, but a few mountain sheep are seen, it was in the wildest part of the canyon that the other cave was found, in fact we almost fell into it. The high grass about the opening hid the dished out entrance.*

"We were at an elevation of approximately 7000 feet and going was tough, especially with a pack, and we had stopped to rest when one of the party remarked that it 'sounded hollow' when any of us talked. Of course, we all yapped away at the same time trying to figure if this was so, and sure enough it was. Further investigation located the hole some six feet to the left of where we had stopped. It was roughly oval in shape, some 30 by 18 feet; and bridged in the center the short way by a natural rock arch heavy enough to support an elephant. In the center of the arch were 3 deep grooves caused we hazarded, by rope passing over the arch. We spent several hours in investigating the surrounding terrain to see if there might be any other entrances to the cave, but found none. It sloped sharply from the opening down about 200 feet, and then the bore disappeared, curving upward. We succeeded in getting down to the first level, by tying all our ropes together, and subsequently investigated a lot of it.

"Threading through the soil were long stringers of quartz, but oddly enough at the same time there were chunks of rock as big as a piano that were solid masses of seashells. Quite a lot of pottery both broken and whole, was found. The most interesting thing was, however, that the farther we went the colder it got. Also there was a sound of either rushing wind or water, which got louder the lower we went. We came upon two human skeletons not over 500 feet from the entrance, but they must have been very old, as the bones crumbled at the touch. Everything was covered with a deep dust after passing the bend and no indication of any living thing having passed there was ever noted.

It was very dark and depressing, and the chill was very penetrating. When you consider that the outside temperature was near 100 degrees, you can imagine how we were dressed.

"We had three flashlights, one a five cell, and after a while it was all that was left that would give a decent light. Down at what we estimated as 1200 feet from the opening we came smack up against a smooth stone wall. That was it. The end. None of us would admit it was natural, it was too smooth and perfect, and look as we would we could not find a single flaw or crack in it. It was of a marble-like texture and some eight or nine feet high in the center and around eleven wide. By placing our ears to the rock surface THE ROARING ON THE OTHER SIDE BECAME MUCH LOUDER, AND THE ROCK WAS QUITE COLD TO THE TOUCH. There was natural marble near there, in Marble Canyon, where marble was once taken out in large quantities, and so the rock was native rock, I'm sure. Since the remaining light was all we had except matches, we voted to get back to the opening as soon as possible, and after a hard struggle upgrade we got back to daylight and held a conference. We decided to bed down and talk it over further the next day, as it was getting late.

"However, the next day we were inclined to look foolishly at each other and claim it was all our imagination thinking there was anything strange on the other side of the barrier, and it was just another one of those many caves in the country. Carlsbad is just 65 miles north of there, AND THE WHOLE COUNTRY IS NO DOUBT HONEYCOMBED UNDERNEATH.

"We finished our experiments and left, late in July but I have never been able to forget the caves, and THE ODD SOUNDS ON THE OTHER SIDE OF THAT BARRIER. Or for that matter, the barrier itself, for it was too perfect to be natural, I believe. Or, maybe I've just read too many AMAZING STORIES,' and am inclined to wild ideas. As the Mexicans say, Quien sabe?

"Some day I'm going to write you a ding-how Scientifiction on something-or-other, and then place it and my rejection notice among

my souvenirs. Maybe then I can go on reading AMAZING STORIES in peace, without wanting to dash off a dinger.

"K. A. Gookin., Carmel Radio & Sound Service., Box 1865., Carmel, California."(136)

◇◇

In a letter appearing in issue No. 14 of *The Shaver Mystery Club Letterzine,* Vaughn M. Greene spoke of a possible 'entrance' to cavern systems near the bottom of the elevator landing in the Hoover dam near Las Vegas, which holds back Lake Mead. Early construction workers allegedly broke into (and probably re-sealed) large caverns while blasting out the cliffs near the base of the dam.(142) In the lower elevator landing, according to Mr. Greene, there was a "wild tile inlay on the floor, with signs of the zodiac and all sorts of stuff suggesting an entrance." He suggests a possible connection between this and the caverns which the workers broke into.(142)

In a 1973 article "Amateur Explorer Discovers Vast Cavern System Containing Underground River Of Gold," David Klein related the discovery of an unusual cavern system located some 300 miles northwest of Vancouver, British Columbia.(143) Allegedly, the caverns contained large amounts of gold, huge unidentifiable human or Sasquatch-like footprints, white-albino frogs, perfectly round stones, and flowing underground rivers. These findings, according to the article, were immediately suppressed by the Canadian government soon after word of the discovery got out.(143)

Chapter 5

The *Ramayana,* one of the most famous texts of India, tells the story of the great avatar, Rama, "an emissary from Agartha" who arrived on a beautiful Vimana (flying chariot).(90) In India, there is an ancient belief, still held by many, of a subterranean race of serpent people who dwelt in the cities Patala and Bhogavati.(90) In Indian religions, Patala denotes the subterranean realms where lower beings, such as nagas, vetalas and asuras reside. According to the legend, they wage war on the kingdom of Agartha.(92) The Nagas are, according to *The Deep Dwellers:*

◇◇

"Described as a very advanced race or species, with a highly developed technology. They also harbor a disdain for human beings, whom they are said to abduct, torture, interbreed with and even to eat."(92)

◇◇

While the entrance to Bhogavati is said to be somewhere in the Himalayas,(91) some believers assert that Patala can be entered through the Well of Sheshna in Benares, India.(90) In *The Deep Dwellers*, William Michael Mott tells us:

"This entrance is very real, with forty steps which descend into a circular depression, to terminate at a closed stone door which is covered in bas-relief cobras."(92)

Figure 62: Stone sculptures of a Naga in Karnataka, India

Naga is the Sanskrit and Pali word for a deity, or class of being, taking the form of a very great snake, found in Hinduism, Buddhism, and Jainism - specifically the king cobra (hooded snake).(91)

Stories involving the Nagas are still very much a part of contemporary cultural traditions, predominantly in the Hindu regions of Asia (India, Nepal, and Bali). In the great epic Mahabharata, the depiction of Nagas tends toward the negative. It calls them the "persecutors of all creatures", and tells us that "the snakes were of virulent poison, great prowess and excess of strength." The great epic frequently characterizes Nagas as having a mixture of human and serpent-like traits.(90)

Communities where the inhabitants consider themselves genetic descendants of Nagas, they conduct expensive and grand rituals to honor these objects of great reverence. The Nairs of Kerala and the ethnically related Tulu Bunts of Karnataka, are clans who believe themselves to have originated from the serpent dynasty.(90)

Vishnu is originally portrayed sheltered or reclining by a giant snake, but this iconography has extended to other deities as well. The serpent is common in Ganesha iconography, appearing around the neck, as a belt, held in a hand, coiled at the ankles, or as a throne. Shiva is also often shown with a snake.(90)

Traditions about Nagas are also very common in the Buddhist countries of Asia. In many countries, the Naga concept has merged with the local traditions of great and wise serpents, or dragons.(90) In Tibet, the Naga was said to dwell in lakes or underground streams and guard treasure. In China, the Naga was equated with the dragon.(91)

The Buddhist Naga generally has the form of a great cobra-like snake, usually with a single head, but sometimes with many. Nagas are portrayed, in Buddhist paintings, as human-like, with a snake or dragon extending over his head. They are believed to inhabit various parts of the earth, primarily dwelling in deep underground caverns.(90)

For Malay sailors, Nagas are a type of many-headed dragon; in Thailand and Java, the Naga is a wealthy underworld deity. In Laos, they are considered sea-faring, or water serpents. In Javanese culture, a Naga is a crowned giant magical serpent, sometimes winged.(90)

In a Cambodian legend, the Naga were a noble reptilian race of beings who possessed a large empire in the Pacific Ocean region. The Naga King's daughter married an Aryan and from their union sprang the Cambodian people. Therefore, Cambodians still say that they are "born from Naga".

The Seven-Headed Naga serpents, depicted as statues on Cambodian temples such as Angkor Wat, represent the seven races within Naga society. This social caste system has a mythological, or symbolic, association with the "seven colors of the rainbow".(90)

An Angami Naga tribal legend from North-East India claims that their ancient ancestors emerged from a subterranean land inside the earth. The Nagas, according to some traditional accounts, are a very advanced race or species, with highly developed technology. They also harbor a disdain for human beings, whom they are said to abduct, torture, interbreed with and even eat.(93) William Michael Mott writes in *The Deep Dwellers*:

◇◇◇

"According to herpetologist and author Sherman A. Minton, as stated in his book Venomous Reptiles, this entrance is very real, with forty steps which descend into a circular depression, to terminate at a

closed stone door which is covered in bas-relief cobras. In Tibet, there is a major mystical shrine also called 'Patala,' which is said by the people there to sit atop an ancient cavern and tunnel system, which reaches throughout the Asian continent and possibly beyond. The Nagas also have an affinity with water, and the entrances to their underground palaces are often said to be hidden at the bottom of wells, deep lakes and rivers."(92)

In "The Hollow Earth: Myth or Reality," published in *Atlantis Rising*, Brad Steiger writes about the "Old Ones,"(94) an ancient, forgotten race that populated the surface world many ages ago and then moved underground:

"The Old Ones, an immensely intelligent and scientifically advanced race have chosen to structure their own environment under the surface of the planet and manufacture all their necessities. The Old Ones are hominid, extremely long-lived, and generally remain aloof from the surface peoples, but from time to time, they have been known to offer constructive criticism; and it has been said, they often kidnap human children to tutor and rear as their own."(94)

Reed Flute Cave, known as the "Palace of Natural Arts," is located in southern China. According to a legend, Reed Flute Cave got its name because the reeds by the cave's mouth could be made into flutes. The limestone cave offers a majestic fairyland of stalactites, stalagmites, stone pillars, stone curtains, birds, plants and animals in fantastic shapes and colors. (95)

Figure 63: Flute Reed Cave, China

Inside, there are more than 70 inscriptions in ink, which date back as far as 792 AD in the Tang Dynasty. These aged inscriptions tell us that it has been an attraction in Guilin since ancient times. The cave is about 240 meters long and a tour currently lasts about one hour.(95)

Figure 64: Flute Reed Cave Stalactites and Stalagmites

The interior of the cave is a veritable show gallery of gorgeous geological formations, created by thousands of years of water erosion on the soft limestone. The walls also consist of beautifully rippling, eroded patterns which have dripped into the rock over millennia.(95)

Today, countless multi-colored lights dramatically illuminate the Reed Flute Cave. The lights are hidden in the cracks and crevices of the space, and the effect is almost surreal, as the lights turn the otherwise dark space into a strange mix of bright neon colors and rough natural shades.

Figure 65: The Great Cave of Niah located in Malaysia

The Niah Great Cave at Niah National Park, in Borneo, contains the oldest remains of homo sapiens found in Borneo, and features the world's largest limestone cave entrance, as well as ancient rock paintings. Recent studies have shown evidence of hominin activity and habitation at the Niah caves from ca. 46,000 to ca. 34,000 years ago.

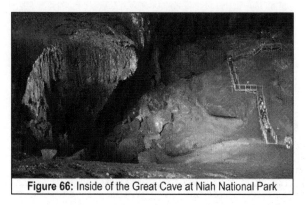

Figure 66: Inside of the Great Cave at Niah National Park

In 1958, a team of archaeologists discovered a 40,000 year old skull. This evidence conflicted with the then accepted idea that Borneo had been settled much later than that.(96) Evidence of continual habitation over the last 40,000 years continues to be unearthed at the caves. There is also speculation that there are tunnels reaching far deeper into the earth.(96)

The Philippines, a Southeast Asian country in the Western Pacific, comprises more than 7,000 islands. The Puerto Princesa Underground River is located in a jungle covered mountain range on the northern coast of the Philippine island of Palawan. It is 8.2 kilometer (5 miles) long and winds through a spectacular cave system before emptying into the South China Sea.

Figure 67: The Puerto Princesa Underground River

The river does a good job of hiding itself. The entrance is in a stone cliff, half submerged by a saltwater lake that feeds directly to the ocean. This entrance is the only clue to the existence of the tunnel beyond. And what stretches out in the darkness is quite remarkable.

Figure 68: Puerto Princesa Underground River, Philippines

The subterranean river extends for miles, completely underground, with unique rock formations all the way along. It winds along and sometimes divides in two, sometimes with smaller streams shooting off. The height of the cave varies. As one travels through it, at one moment it appears quite low and, at the next, the cave opens up into a grand chamber towering over 60 meters high.

Figure 69: The Puerto Princesa Underground River

It is only permitted to go about 1.5 kilometers along the river even though the caves stretch out for another six or seven kilometers. The 45 minute round trip is enough to get a great sense of the site, however one can not help but wonder what lies down past where the tourists are not allowed to venture.

There are rumors of cavern entrances, which flow down into even deeper and larger rivers, which one can navigate, until they empty into a huge underground lake.

Majlis al Jinn (Arabic for "meeting/gathering place of the Jinn") is recognized as one of the largest underground caves in the world, and located in a remote area of the Selma Plateau in Oman.(97)

Majlis al Jinn is a single cave chamber measuring about 310 meters by 225 meters (1,017 by 738 feet), with a domed ceiling 120 meters (393 feet) high. The maximum temperature inside the cave is between 17-18° C (62-64° F). (97)

Figure 70: Majlis al Jinn (Arabic: "meeting place of the Jinn")

The deepest part of the cave is 178 meters (584 feet) below the top. To put its size into perspective: 12 Boeing 747 jumbo planes would fit inside the cave chamber. The cave is currently only for experienced climbers, but there are some plans to develop the deeper parts into a more easily accessible tourist site.(97)

Until fairly recently there had not been a way to reach the cave by car, so spelunkers had to hike in, carrying their equipment, or rent donkeys from a village a few hours walk from the cave entrance.(97)

The original explorers, Don and Cheryl, often flew into the area by helicopter. Now, there is a rough track, which requires four-wheel drive, which goes to the cave.(98)

Figure 71: Majlis Al Jinn Cave, Selma Plateau in Oman

There are three different entrances to the Majlis al Jinn cave, all of which link to a single enormous chamber. The local legend tells of a beautiful woman named Selma, who inhabited in the cave many years ago. An enormous, one-eyed genie (Jinn) persued Selma. He was extremely angry with her.

She ran for her life across the plateau, as the Jinn chased her, while hurling lightning bolts at her. Fortunately for Selma, the Jinn's depth perception was not very good, since it possessed one eye. Three lightning bolts went astray, fracturing the earth and creating the cave entrances we know today.(97,98)

The Jeita grotto, the longest explored cave in Lebanon, consists of two separate, but interconnected, karstic limestone caves: the upper and lower grotto. The upper gallery houses the world's largest stalactite - a mineral deposit that hangs from the ceiling of a limestone cave The lower gallery which has an overall length of 6,200 meters (20,300 feet) is located 60 meters (200 feet) below the upper gallery. It is traversed by a smooth underwater river and a lake.(99)

Figure 72: Jeita grotto is the longest explored cave in Lebanon

In 1958, Lebanese archeologists discovered the upper galleries, 60 meters (200 ft) above the lower cave. They have since been accommodated with an access tunnel, and a series of walkways, to enable safe access for tourists, without disturbing the natural landscape. The upper galleries house the world's largest known stalactite. The galleries are composed of a series of chambers the largest of which peaks at a height of 120 meters (390 ft).(99)

The Jeita cave emits a life-sustaining spring, which provides fresh drinking water for the one-and-a-half million inhabitants of the capital, Beirut. Initially referred to as the Grottoes of Nahr al-Kalb, it was subsequently known as Djaita, Jehita, and finally Jeita. Naher el Kalb is the name of the river that runs through the grottoes, while Jeita, meaning "roaring water" in Aramaic, is the town in which the cave's entrance is located. The transition from Grottoes of Nahr al-Kalb to Jeita Grottoes occurred in 1927, as newspapers widely used the latter name. (99)

Chapter 6

Measuring over 1,000 miles from southwest to northeast and 500 miles from north to south, the Gobi is a vast desert in Asia, spanning from northern China to southern Mongolia. This massive desert basin is nestled between the Altai Mountains on the north, the Taklamakan Desert to the West, the Tibetan Plateau to the southwest, and the North China Plain to the southeast.

Once part of the great Mongol Empire, and located prominently along the famous Silk Road, the Gobi desert has an even more ancient and mysterious occult history of subterranean worlds which is now re-surfacing.

Figure 73: The Gobi Desert, China

The Gobi has several Chinese names, including Shamo, a generic term for desert, and Hanhai, which means "endless sea". Mu is the most popular name given to the legendary empire on the surface of what is now the Gobi desert. Following major cataclysms which left the desert in its current condition, the inhabitants of Mu were said to have taken refuge in underground cities, which they had terraformed inside of gigantic natural caves and caverns.

The Tibetans call these cities Agartha and Shambhala, having believed for millennia that they serve as reservoirs of ancient knowledge and advanced technology. Madam Blavatsky, the foundress of Theosophy, describes Shambhala in her *Secret Doctrine*:

"In the same manner and on the plan of the Zodiac in the upper Ocean or the heavens, a certain realm on Earth, an island sea, was consecrated and called "the Abyss of Learning"; twelve centers on it in the shape of twelve small islands representing the Zodiacal signs - two of which remained for ages the "mystery signs" and were the abodes of twelve Hierophants and masters of wisdom. This "sea of knowledge" or learning remained for ages there, where now stretches the Shamo or Gobi desert. It existed until the last great glacial period, when a local cataclysm, which swept the waters south and west and so formed the present great desolate desert, left only a certain oasis, with a lake and one island in the midst of it, as a relic of the Zodiacal Ring on Earth." (100)

According to Ignatious Donnelly, in *Atlantis the Antediluvian World*, during the Pleistocene (ice age), the gods of the ancients were members of a superhuman race, who ruled Atlantis and governed ordinary humans.

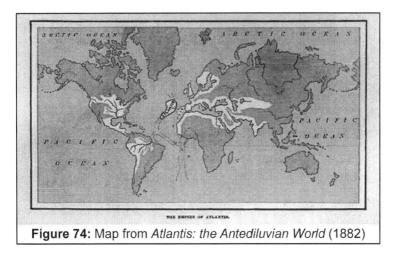

Figure 74: Map from *Atlantis: the Antediluvian World* (1882)

Before the cataclysmic destruction of their continent, which they had foreseen as sea levels had risen from melting ice, they took refuge in the honeycombed interior caverns of the Earth. They have continued to live there ever since.

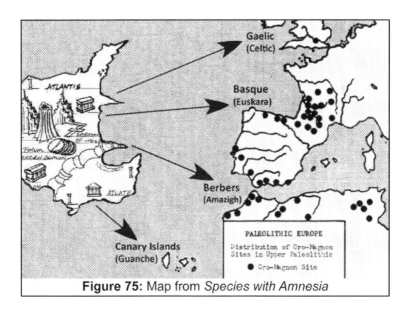

Figure 75: Map from *Species with Amnesia*

Blavatsky, for the most part, agrees that the Atlantean capital is in the Atlantic. She also refers to an island from one remote time in the past. Blavatsky says:

"What is claimed is simply the fact that the Wisdom imparted by the "Divine Ones" has remained in all its pristine purity in a certain Brotherhood. The said School or Fraternity being closely connected with a certain island of an inland sea, believed in by both Hindus and Buddhists, but called "mythical" by geographers and Orientalists, the less one talks of it, the wiser he will be." (101)

Blavatsky alludes to an ancient island location:

"The "Island," according to belief, exists to the present hour; now, as an oasis surrounded by the dreadful wildernesses of the great Desert, the Gobi - whose sands "no foot hath crossed in the memory of man"."(102) "the mystery name of that region which extends from Kailas mountain nearly to the Schamo Desert - from within which the Kalki Avatar is expected."(102)

Figure 76: Madame Helena P. Blavatsky

Blavatsky mentions this expected avatar once more:

"Shambhala, a very mysterious locality on account of its future associations. A town or village mentioned in the Puranas, whence, it is prophesied, the Kalki Avatar will appear. The "Kalki" is Vishnu, the Messiah on the White Horse of the Brahmins; Maitreya Buddha of the Buddhists, Sosiosh of the Parsis, and Jesus of the Christians (See Revelations). All these "messengers" are to appear "before the destruction of the world", says the one; before the end of Kali Yuga say the others. It is in S'ambhala that the future Messiah will be born. Some Orientalists make modern Muradabad in Rohilkhand (N.W.P.) identical with S'ambhala, while Occultism places it in the Himalayas. It is pronounced Shambhala." (103)

According to the general belief, it is situated in north-west Tibet. Some place it within the unexplored central regions, inaccessible even to the fearless nomadic tribes; others hem it in between the Gangdisri Mountains and the northern edge of the Gobi Desert, on the south and north, and in between the more populated regions of Khoondooz and Kashmir, of the Gya-Pheling (British-India), and China, on the west and east, which affords a pretty large latitude in which the curious mind might locate it.

Others place it between Namur Nur and the Kuen-Lun Mountains – but one and all firmly believe in Schambhala, and speak of it as a fertile, fairy-like land, once an island, now an oasis of incomparable beauty, the place of meeting of the inheritors of the esoteric wisdom of the god-like inhabitants of the legendary island." (104)

In an article for *Atlantis Rising*, entitled, *The Hollow Earth: Myth or Reality*, Brad Steiger describes some legends pertaining to these subterranean inhabitants:

"The Old Ones are an ancient race that populated the surface world, who then moved underground. They are an immensely intelligent and scientifically advanced race that have chosen to structure their

own environment under the surface of the planet and manufacture all their necessities. The Old Ones are hominid, extremely long-lived, and predate Homo sapiens. They generally remain aloof from the surface peoples, but from time to time, they have been known to offer constructive criticism; and it has been said, they often kidnap human children to tutor and rear as their own."(94)

◇◇

In Tibet, a major mystical shrine called 'Patala,' is rumored to sit on top of an ancient cavern and subterranean tunnel system, which reaches throughout the Asian continent and possibly beyond.

Buddhist legend holds that a race of supermen and superwomen reside there. They occasionally come to the surface to oversee the development of the human race. This incredible underground oasis supposedly has millions of inhabitants and numerous connected cities.(94)

Beneath southern China's landscape researchers have discovered some of the largest underground chambers in the world. One huge cave system in the Chongqing Province is so large that it has clouds, fog, streams and lots of vegetation.(105)

Figure 77: Er Wang Dong, cave system in Chongqing, China, so massive that it has its own weather system.

Caves, which form naturally by the weathering of rock, often extend very deep underground, and open up into enormous caverns. Agartha is a legendary subterranean civilization that is said to reside miles under the Earth's crust, in extensive honeycomb caverns. Shamballa (also known as Shambalah or Shangri-La) is sometimes referred to as its capital city.(94)

The mythical paradise of Shamballa is known by many different names: It has been called the Forbidden Land, the Land of White Waters, the Land of Radiant Spirits, the Land of Living Fire, the Land of the Living Gods and the Land of Wonders.(94)

Hindus have called it as Aryavartha (literally: Realm of the Aryans; Land of the Noble Ones") - the land from which the Vedas come; the Chinese name it Hsi Tien, the Western Paradise of Hsi Wang Mu, the Royal Mother of the West; the Russian Old Believers, a nineteenth-century Christian sect, knew it as Belovodye and the Kirghiz people called it Janaidar. But throughout Asia it is best known by its Sanskrit name, Shambhala, meaning 'the place of peace, of tranquility.'(94)

In 1992, 24 man-made caves were discovered in China, displaying incredible craftsmanship that involved the excavation of 36,000 cubic meters of stone. The floor of the grotto was more than two thousand square meters, with the tallest point exceeding 30 meters. There are no historical references to these caves, and the reason they were built is still uncertain.

Figure 78-a: Longyou Caves, China

In his book, *On the Shores of Endless Worlds*, Andrew Tomas provides another perspective on an ancient myth:

"According to legend, King Minos of Crete ordered his architect Daedalus to construct the labyrinth, a maze of passages so

113

ingeniously devised that even the builder himself could not find his way without a plan. In the center lived the Minotaur, half bull, half human, to whom the Greeks sent seven youths and seven maidens as a tribute every nine years.

"The Minotaur was slain by Theseus who was able to find his way out of the labyrinth thanks to a ball of thread given to him by Ariadne. This myth has been interpreted as an historical record of the construction of the palace of Minos in Knossos which contains innumerable galleries and rooms. On the other hand, this myth may have an entirely different interpretation, similar to a cryptogram, which conceals the existence of a secret repository of underground chambers and passages..."(148)

Archaeologists working in Turkey have recently broken through into a vast underground labyrinth system, which could be compared in size to a small modern city. Although several of these 'cities' have been found, the largest seems to lie beneath the city of Derinkuyu.(147)

Figure 78-b: Subterranean tunnel below Derinkuyu, Turkey

Extending to a depth of approximately 60 meters (200 feet), Derinkuyu is large enough to have sheltered as many as 20,000 people together with their livestock.(147) The subterranean cavern-systems there are quite extensive, consisting of many levels and caverns, and in some places are connected by tunnels only 3 or 4 feet in diameter.(146) Were these miniature tunnels constructed this way for defensive purposes, or for inhabitants of a very short stature? According to tradition, many of these troglodyte cave-cities were utilized by early Christians escaping persecution. It is not known, however, whether the Christians built the cities, or whether these huge underground villages are of a much more ancient origin.

In his article, "Underground Civilization Attacks German Archaeologists," Kurt Braun recounts how some men who were exploring the lower depths of the Derenkuyu labyrinth were allegedly attacked physically, by a tall, albino-like race of humans.(146) Since most of the underground 'cities' have not been fully explored, it is uncertain just how extensive they are, or how deep down below the surface the tunnel systems descend. The underground city at Derinkuyu was opened to visitors in 1969, and about half of the underground city is currently accessible to tourists.

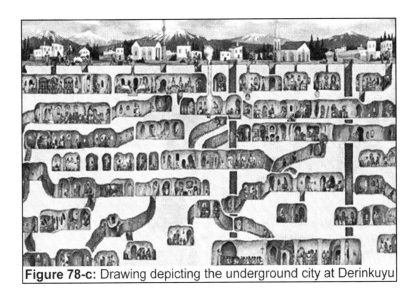

Figure 78-c: Drawing depicting the underground city at Derinkuyu

Chapter 7

In her 1982 article "Odyssey Into Egypt", Dr. Earlyne Chaney describes a discovery that she claims to have witnessed in Egypt, along with researcher Bill Cox. They were allegedly shown two tunnels, neither of which had been fully explored.(141) One was in the Temple of Edfu, located on the west bank of the Nile, between Luxor and Cairo, in the ruins of El Tuna Gabel. The other was near Zoser's Step Pyramid, in Cairo near Memphis-Saqqarah, located within the tomb of the Bull (called Serapium).

According to the article, the Egyptian government sealed both tunnels after some of their archaeologists claimed that the entrances "lead too deeply down into the depths of the earth," and that they found the crust to be "honeycombed with passages leading off into other depths."(141) The Egyptian authorities concluded that the possibility of explorers becoming lost was too great, according to Dr. Chaney, so access to the tunnels has been restricted and remain off-limits.(142)

At the Earth's Core, a 1914 fantasy novel by Edgar Rice Burroughs, is the first in his series about the subject of a hollow Earth, an inhabited land called Pellucidar.(106) A man traveling in the Sahara Desert encounters a mining heir with an experimental excavating machine called the "iron mole." It burrows 500 miles into the Earth's crust, emerging into the unknown interior world. The novel was filmed as *At the Earth's Core* in 1976.

In this adventure, the Earth is a hollow shell, with people living in massive cities within the shell. The subterranean world also features prehistoric creatures of all geological eras, and is dominated by a race of reptilian humanoids. The reptilians enslave the subterranean humans, and use an ape-like hybrid simian race as slaves.(106)

Figure 79: Iron Mole from *At the Earth's Core*

Tarzan at the Earth's Core, another novel by Edgar Rice Burroughs, involves a scientist who has discovered the interior world at the Earth's center. Tarzan uses a German Zeppelin, to enter the Earth, where he encounters massive internal seas, prehistoric reptiles, and a breakaway human civilization .(107)

Figure 80: *Tarzan at the Earth's Core* cover by David B. Mattingly

Leaving his relatively safe home in the African jungle to answer the call to great adventure, Tarzan of the Apes joins an expedition to the Arctic to seek an opening in the earth's surface that leads to the inner world. (107)

Figure 81-a: Germany had many blimps in use during World War I

Sailing on a German-made blimp, they glide almost imperceptibly from our world into the strange, mysterious and often terrifying land that lies beneath the earth's crust. When they arrive, neither Tarzan's jungle lore nor the charts of scientists are of any use as they face the problem of rescuing an American adventurer who is held captive by blood-thirsty inner earth inhabitants.(107)

A ferocious bat-like creature carries Tarzan away in its talons, but he manages to escape. He slashes his way through trackless forests and dangerous swamps, and outwitting his cruel captors. Tarzan faces the most terrific encounter of his adventure-crammed life when, rescuing the beautiful Jana, known as the "Red Flower", he falls into the hands of reptile-men who move with lightning speed and relentless ferocity to spread terror throughout the land.(107) How much of these fictional stories could be based on truth?

Richard Hinckley Allen explains in his 1899 book, *In Star Names and Their Meanings*, that the Great Sphinx of Giza was constructed "with Virgo's head on Leo's body, from the fact that the sun passed through these two constellations during the inundation of the Nile." The Great Sphinx aligns perfectly toward cardinal east, reflecting the significance of the four cardinal directions in the Old Kingdom. (108)

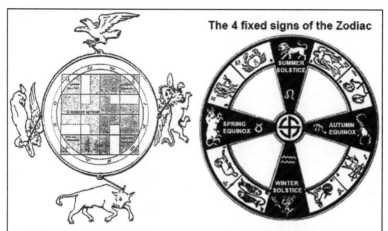

Figure 81-b: A 26,000 year cycle known as the precession of the equinoxes as the root cause of the astrological ages.

During the process of mummification, the four organs consisting of the liver, lungs, stomach and intestines, were placed by the Egyptians in special containers called canopic jars. The jars were personified by four different gods, known as the Sons of Horus, and were associated with the four cardinal compass points.(40)

Figure 81-c: Ancient Egyptian canopic jars, personified as the Sons of Horus, which accompanied mummified bodies.

According to E.C. Krupp, the cardinal directions originate astronomically in the daily rotation of the sky around the north celestial pole, which was a location of high religious and occult importance to the ancient Egyptians, as the entire Giza necropolis adheres to an accurate cardinal grid.(109)

Figure 82: Aerial view of the Great Sphinx at Giza, Egypt

The Giza Plateau in Egypt has an enormous underground system that is a combination of man made caverns and tunnels as well as subterranean rivers and passages. Since 1978, these caverns have been mapped using ground penetrating radar, and explored on expeditions led by Dr. Jim Hurtak, who has entered gigantic chambers, some larger than our largest cathedrals.(110)

A few historians have suggested that the underground cave system at Giza, is the legendary 'City of the Gods', the massive underground city described by Herodotus in the 5th century BC:

There I saw twelve palaces regularly disposed, which had communication with each other, interspersed with terraces and arranged around twelve halls. It is hard to believe they are the work of man. The walls are covered with carved figures, and each court is exquisitely built of white marble and surrounded by a colonnade. Near the corner where the labyrinth ends, there is a pyramid, two hundred and forty feet in height, with great carved figures of animals on it and an underground passage by which it can be entered. I was told very credibly that underground chambers and passages connected this pyramid with the pyramids at Memphis.(111)

Furthermore, he spoke of a multi-level megalithic metropolis under Giza that was thousands of years old.(111) Many ancient writers supported Herodotus' record of underground passages connecting major pyramids. Lamblichus, a fourth-century Syrian representative of the Alexandrian School of mystical and philosophical studies, wrote about an entrance way through the body of the Sphinx into the Great Pyramid:

"This entrance, obstructed in our day by sands and rubbish, may still be traced between the forelegs of the crouched colossus. It was formerly closed by a bronze gate whose secret spring could be operated only by the Magi. It was guarded by public respect, and a sort of religious fear maintained its inviolability better than armed protection would have done.

"In the belly of the Sphinx were cut out galleries leading to the subterranean part of the Great Pyramid. These galleries were so artfully crisscrossed along their course to the Pyramid that, in setting forth into the passage without a guide throughout this network, one inevitably returned to the starting point.(114)

Since the declassification of the ground penetrating radar, more and more underground systems have been discovered in various places around the world, systems that remain unexplored.

Figure 83: Aerial view of a stone church in Lalibela, Ethiopia

Lalibela is one of Ethiopia's holiest cities, famous for monolithic churches carved entirely out of volcanic rock. Egypt's pyramids are commonly considered the continent's top man-made attractions, however, these far lesser-known semi-underground churches are among the most impressive sights in all of Africa.

No stone was added to the structures during in construction; the volcanic rock was carved away leaving behind these magnificent cross shaped buildings. Expert carvers painstakingly hollowed the rock to create large chambers, complete with ornate religious sculptures.(113)

The Portuguese priest Francisco Álvares (1465–1540) visit to Lebna Dengel in the 1520s and described the unique church structures as follows:

"I weary of writing more about these buildings, because it seems to me that I shall not be believed if I write more...I swear by God, in Whose power I am, that all I have written is the truth" (114)

Figure 84: Subterranean church in Lalibela, Ethiopia

There is some controversy as to when Ethiopia's nearly 200 rock-hewn churches were constructed, though mainstream archeologists generally accept that the eleven churches at Lalibela were constructed in several phases, between the seventh and thirteenth centuries.(113)

Ethiopian tradition ascribes the whole complex's construction to the reign of King Gebre Mesqel Lalibela (ca. 1181‑1221). According to the king's hagiography (gadl), they were carved over a period of twenty-four years, with the assistance of "angels".(113)

Figure 85: Ancient swastika-style cross windows, Lalibela, Ethiopia

The churches occupy pits, roughly the size of tennis courts, scooped from the surrounding earth. A few of them are linked by underground tunnels, which connect them via passages that are hidden from the surface.(114) It almost looks as if the churches were dropped into the pits that contain them. Though called "underground churches," the sky is visible. Outside the churches, monks live in caves in the pit walls.

Some oral legends maintain that these subterranean shrines lead to deeper passages, which if followed deep enough, lead to an underground inhabited world.(113) It is not entirely clear who the inhabitants of this inner word are, if it exists, but some have claimed that it could be of another species, perhaps reptilian.(115)

Figure 86-a: Credo Mutwa, South Africa

Zulu "Sanusi" (diviner or sangoma) Credo Mutwa is a man whom researcher David Icke describes as: "a friend, a genius."(116) While not formally educated, many consider Credo Mutwa a living encyclopedia of ancient African wisdom and a keeper of oral legend. He is the author of many books, including *Song of the Stars: The Lore of a Zulu Shaman*, *Indaba, My Children* and *Zulu Shaman: Dreams, Prophecies, and Mysteries*. According to Mutwa:

"The people of Rwanda, the Hutu people, as well as the Watusi people, state, and they are not the only people in Africa who state this, that their very oldest ancestors were a race of beings whom they called the Imanujela, which means "the Lords who have come". And some tribes in West Africa, such as a Bambara people, also say the same thing."

"The Zulu people, who are famous as a warrior people, the people to whom King Shaka Zulu, of the last century, belonged. The Zulus claim that many, many thousands of years ago a race of people who were like lizards..

"And people married their daughters to them and produced a power race of Kings and tribal Chiefs, there are hundreds of fairy-tales, sir, in which a lizard female assumes the identity of a human princess and poses as her, and gets married to a Zulu Prince. No matter where you go throughout Southern, Eastern, Western, and Central Africa, you'll find that the description of these creatures is the same. Even amongst tribes which never, throughout their long history, had contact with each other at all.

"So, there ARE such creatures. Where they come from, I will never claim to know, sir. It is said that these creatures feed on us human beings. They hide in deep cavities underground, because they are always feeling cold. In these cavities, we are told, there are huge fires which are kept going by slaves, human, zombie-like slaves.

"And, it is further said that these Zuswazi, these Imbulu, or whatever you choose to call them, are not capable of eating solid food.. they eat

human blood. And there is another name by which these creatures are known. This name is Chitauli. Now, the word Chitauli means "the dictators, the ones who tell us the law". In other words, "they who tell us, secretly, what we are to do". Now, it is said that these Chitauli did a number of things to us..

"And, another thing the Chitauli forced human beings to do, they forced human beings to mine into the Earth. The Chitauli activated human women and made them to discover minerals and metals of certain types. Women discovered copper; women discovered gold; women discovered silver. And, eventually, they were guided by the Chitauli to alloy these metals and to create new metals which had never existed in Nature before, metals such as bronze and brass and others.

"Many African tribes believe in what is called Midzimu or Badimo. Now, the word Midzimu or Badimo means "them who are in the sky". But, in Zulu-land, amongst my people, you find this amazing schism going hand-in-hand. There are Zulus who believe that the dead ones are the Abapansi, which means "the ones who are below, who are under the Earth".(115, 116)

⋄⋄

Credo Mutwa also claims that black African tribes had seen tall, blond-haired, blue-eyed beings throughout the continent, long before the white Europeans arrived. According to Credo, the official historian of the Zulu nation, when the Europeans first came, the black Africans thought they were the return of these same white "gods", which they called the Mzungu. As a result they called the European settlers by that name, which is still used today.(116)

This was very much the same reaction that Central American peoples had when Cortes arrived in 1519; they thought he was the returning god, Quetzalcoatl, another god described as tall with blue eyes.(58) He was called Viracocha by the Incas, Kukulkan by the Mayas, Quetzalcoatl by the Aztecs, Gucumatz in Central America, Votan in Palenque and Zamna in Izamal. He and his 'men' were usually described as being bearded with white skin.(58)

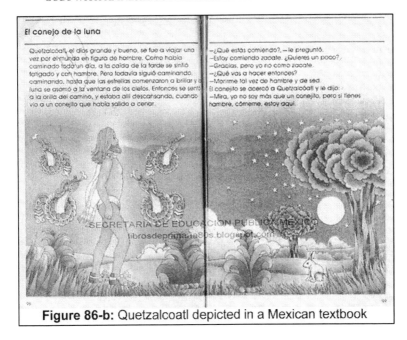

Figure 86-b: Quetzalcoatl depicted in a Mexican textbook

Chapter 8

Snaefellsjökull is a 700,000-year-old volcano, with a glacier covering its summit, in western Iceland. The mountain is one of the most famous sites of Iceland, primarily due to *Journey to the Center of the Earth* (1864) by Jules Verne, in which the protagonists find the entrance to a passage leading to the inner Earth.(117)

The main characters make their way through hazardous passages and survive the tortures of thirst to discover, eighty-eight miles down, a vast sea. What seems to amaze them most after their long ordeal in a series of labyrinthine tunnels is the brightness of the underground world.(117) Declares Axel:

"It was like an aurora borealis, a continuous cosmic phenomenon, filling a cavern big enough to contain an ocean."(117)

Figure 87: Illustrations *Journey to the Center of the Earth* (1864)

There is an inner sun in the novel, different from the sun in our solar system. The inner sun results from the convergence to a point of the cosmic rays that have penetrated Earth. The friction of the rays coming together creates the light.(117)

Figure 88: The Earth bisected centrally, giving a clear view of the central sun, interior continents and oceans

The Norwegian sailor, Olaf Jansen, described the inner sun as "smoky," and it was the basis for the title of the book *"The Smoky God"*. As the Hollow Earth people are not exposed to solar radiation, their lifespans are much longer than people living on the surface.(34) The protagonists construct a raft and sail across this mysterious ocean, discovering a lost world of giant plants and prehistoric reptiles. Throughout, the character of the professor remains the model of a rational, nineteenth-century scientist, as he tries to calculate how the subterranean lake came to be. (117)

He speculates that the ocean had flowed down from the surface through a fissure, which closed, and that some of the vapor had evaporated to cause clouds and storms. The nephew reflects that, "This theory about the phenomenon we had witnessed structured as satisfactory, for however goes the wonders of nature they can always be explained by physical laws."(117)

Spartakus and the Sun Beneath the Sea is a French television series created by Nina Wolmark.(119) The plot revolves around the lost city of Arkadia, the home to an ancient civilization which escaped a great cataclysmic event by relocating deep within the crust. Unaware that any life survived on the surface, the elders sealed all records of their past in the city's Archives in an effort to keep their population safe.(119)

Arkadia is illuminated by a dying, artificial sun. A group of Arkadians defy the law and enter the Archives, and with what they learned about the world above, they create a messenger named Arkana and send her above to find help.(119)

Arkana brings back two kids, through the underground strata (which seem like alternative dimensions), to save Arkadia. They travel in a spaceship called Tehrig, along with Spartakus and Arkadia's animal mascots.(119) Although this animation is primarily targeted towards children, it maintains a mature and candid tone, evident in it's opening narration:

"*Ever since the time of the Great Cataclysm, the Arkadians have lived deep in the center of the Earth. They believed they were the only survivors of this great devastation. Their civilization thrived under the power of their sun, the Tehra...until it began to fail. In desperation, the children of Arkadia broke the law and entered the forbidden Archives, searching for a solution. What they discovered gave them hope. Anxiously, they used their special powers and created a messenger to the people above. They named her Arkana.*"(119)

During the summer of 1998, cave explorers confirmed that a linked cave system some 15 miles in length, winds underneath North Wales.(120) German archaeologist Dr. Heinrich Kusch announced that there is considerable evidence regarding the deep tunnel systems that have been found beneath many prehistoric European settlements. He compared these hidden, or forgotten, tunnels to ancient highways beneath the surface.(120)

Figure 89: Underground tunnel systems found under dozens of European Neolithic settlements. Image by Dr. Heinrich Kush

The empirical evidence of these Stone Age "highways" has recently increased with the discovery and exploration of dozens of Neolithic settlements scattered from Scotland to Turkey.(120) Most of these settlements have been dated to the Late Pleistocene (end of the last ice age). The fact that so many of these ancient networks have survived after 12,000 years indicates that the original tunnels must have been engineered and constructed on a truly massive scale.

In *Secrets Of The Underground Door To An Ancient World*, Dr Heinrich Kusch reveals convincing evidence regarding the many miles of tunnels that he has investigated:

<><><><><><><><><><><><><><><><><><><><><><><><><><><><><><><><><><><><><><><><><><>

"Across Europe there were thousands of them - from the north in Scotland down to the Mediterranean. Most are not much larger than big wormholes - just 70cm wide - just wide enough for a person to wriggle along but nothing else. They are interspersed with nooks, at

some places it's larger and there is seating, or storage chambers and rooms. They do not all link up but taken together it is a massive underground network."(120)

◇◇

Some archeologists believe the network was a way of protecting man from predators. Others maintain that there were periodic cataclysms, from which Europeans took subterranean refuge. Still others believe that some of the linked tunnels functioned as do today; they allowed for people to travel safely regardless of wars, violence, or weather conditions on the surface.(120)

Dr. Heinrich Kusch believes that the Church often built beautiful stone chapels by the entrances, perhaps because it was fearful of the heathen legacy the tunnels might have represented, and wanted to negate their influence.(120) What I found most fascinating were the writings that referred to the tunnels as a gateway to the underworld. According to Dr. Kusch:

◇◇

"In Bavaria in Germany alone we have found 700 meters of these underground tunnel networks. In Syria in Austria we have found 350 meters. Across Europe there were thousands of them - from the north in Scotland down to the Mediterranean. In Spain and North Africa, with others reported even in the Sahara."(120)

◇◇

In an article called *Extensive Ancient Underground Networks Discovered Throughout Europe*, April Holloway compares Dr. Kusch's findings to ancient myths and legends from all over the world that refer to underground cities and tunnels:

◇◇

"According to mythological traditions, underground sites were mostly referred to as entrances to the underworld and we find such references all around the world. Although most of us think of the 'underworld' as a representation of 'hell' and therefore an imaginary

or spiritual place for 'bad' people, in reality in ancient religions that wasn't the case. The underworld was a place where the dead would go, but it was a place with physical entrances, guards, buildings and cities, and a place that a few mortals could visit and even communicate with the dead souls, gods, kings or the armies of the underworld. In a few cases though, according to the legends, they could even resurrect a dead person.

"One of the most famous underground cities is the city of Agartha, a legendary city that is supposed to be in the center of the Earth, the Earth's Core. Central Asia is the origin of those legends and the race inhabiting this underground realm was called the Agharti. Theosophists refer to Agartha as a vast complex of caves and an underground network that was inhabited by the Asuras (evil demons) and enemies of the Gods. This underground network was supposedly made by man.

"In Hindu mythology there are legends of a race called the Nagas, serpent like intelligent creatures with human faces that live in underground caverns. Those creatures are described as 'children of Gods' who got married with human kings and queens and are supposedly spiritually advanced. Similarly, in Chinese legends dragons are not the ugly flying beasts that we believe today, but wise creature that would be mentors of kings and creators of kingdoms. Many Tibetans are mentioned to have entered those caves of the Nagas that expand miles and miles inside the mountains of Asia.

"What is interesting is that a strange light emanates in those underground realms which has also been mentioned as the hollow earth inner sun. So the underground cities are not in dark as we would believe. Some of those realms now are inside Earth while in the past they used to be on the surface but were forced to move inside Earth due to circumstances like attacks or maybe even climate change.

"Shambhala (a Sanskrit word meaning 'place of peace') is another famous holy place that for some is supposed to be a spiritual 'paradise', but for others it is suggested to be a real underground city

with references of people that have actually visited it. Legends mention that the King of Shambhala traveled to India to meet Buddha and listen to his teachings. One major difference with Shambhala is that it is supposed to be a holy place in comparison to Agartha, which is a place of demons. According to Helena Blavatsky, Shambhala is located in the Gobi Desert.

"On the other side of Earth, in America we have the legend of Akakor, a legend that the latest adventure of Indiana Jones and the Crystal Skulls was based on. Tatunca Nara, an Amazon jungle guide, claims to have seen the city and described not only the city but also the chronicles of the underground kingdom. According to that legend 'Gods' came from a solar system known as 'Schwerta' and built an underground tunnel system in South America. This civilization left 13 underground cities in South America in the jungles of Amazon, yet to be found.

"In the Mayan mythology we have the mythical underground city of Xibalba, 'the land that the sun goes down into' which was inhabited by superheroes and Gods, a civilization that supposedly vanished around the Middle Ages. The entrance to this world was thought to be located in Guatemala and description of the structures and locations within Xibalba are described in Popol Vuh.

"In Greece, we have the myths of Hades and the Underworld, a realm where gods and heroes lived. God Pluto was the God of the Underworld which had many different sections including the Elysium and Tartarus.

"In Irish legends we hear about the people named Tuatha De Danaan (People of the Goddess Danu), a race who moved underground when another race arrived on the island. According to the legends they came to Ireland in 'dark clouds' and landed on the mountains of Ireland. Those people in today's myths are referred to as fairies.

"In Norwegian legends we have the Dwarves, beings of the underground associated with craftsmanship. Different races of Dwarves that were the ones that supplied the Gods with weapons.

"In Egypt, we have references of the historians Herodotus and Strabo of a colossal underground temple that contained 3,000 rooms full of paintings and hieroglyphs, a lost labyrinth yet to be found.(121)

In a 2012 article for *Discovery,* called "First Ever Etruscan Pyramids Found in Italy," Rossella Lorenzi reports on what archeologists claim is the first ever Etruscan pyramid located in the city of Orvieto in central Italy.(122)

Carved into the rock of the Tufa plateau, a sedimentary area resulting from of volcanic activity, on which the city stands, the subterranean structures were largely filled and had to be carefully unearthed. Only the top-most modern layer was visible at the start. Much progress has been made at the Italian site. David B. George of the Department of Classics at Saint Anselm explained:

"Within this upper section, which had been modified in modern times and was used as a wine cellar, we noticed a series of ancient stairs carved into the wall. They were clearly of Etruscan construction"(122)

Figure 90: Ancient structures discovered in Orvieto, Italy

As archeologists started digging, they noticed that the cave's walls tapered up, in a pyramidal fashion. A series of tunnels ran underneath hinting at the likelihood of much deeper, yet undiscovered, structures below. After going through a mid-20th century floor and wine cellar, archeologists continued through a medieval floor. Immediately beneath this floor, they discovered a layer containing various ancient Etruscan artifacts from the middle of the 6th and 5th century B.C. with inscriptions, as well as various objects that dated to before 1000 B.C. Digging through this layer, the archaeologists found 5 feet of gray sterile fill, which had intentionally been deposited from a hole in the top of the structure.(122)

Co-director of the excavation Claudio Bizzarri of the Parco Archeologico Ambientale dell'Orvietano noted that there are at least five pyramids under the city.(122) Three of these structures have yet to be excavated. According to Bizzarri:

"Below that material there was a brown layer that we are currently excavating. Intriguingly, the stone carved stairs run down the wall as we continue digging. We still don't know where they are going to take us. At this level we found a tunnel running to another pyramidal structure and dating from before the 5th century B.C. which adds to the mystery. Clearly, they are not quarries or cisterns. I would say that there is nothing like these structures on record anywhere in Italy. Most likely, the answer waits at the bottom. The problem is we don't really know how much we have to dig to get down there."(122)

Indeed, the Etruscans have long been considered one of antiquity's greatest enigmas, especially since WW2, when the term "Aryan" was literally expunged from academia, and therefore erased from recorded history.(40)

Often depicted as blond on Roman frescoes and mosaics, the Etruscan people were known for their art, agriculture, fine metal-working and commerce. They were documented as being a fun-loving, aesthetically orientated, and altruistic people, who taught the French how to make wine, the Romans how to build roads, and introduced the art of writing to most of Europe.(123)

They flourished in Etruria (an area in central Italy that covered what now are Tuscany, Latium, Emilia-Romagna and Umbria) around 900 B.C., dominated much of the country for five centuries, and started to decline during the fifth century B.C., as the Romans grew in power. By 300-100 B.C., they became absorbed into the Roman empire, which sank into multicultural decline.(123)

Their language had affinities to Latin and other Aryan languages, but was virtually extinguished as they left no literature to document their society. Most of what we know about them comes from other civilizations, or from their cemeteries: their richly decorated tombs.(40) Their origins are still being debated as more discoveries are made, especially across Europe.

In the NY Times article "Underground Tunnels Threaten Town in Hungary's Wine Country," Malcolm W. Browne tells of over 60 miles of ancient tunnel systems of unknown origin and purpose, some of which have collapsed, which have been discovered beneath the town of Eger, Hungary.(137) The civilization which constructed the tunnels must have been fairly advanced in engineering in order to create such a vast subterranean system.

The Bosnian Valley of the Pyramids is a controversial archeological site discovered by Dr. Semir Osmanagic. Below the site, there exists an extensive network of underground tunnels and chambers. These tunnels run for several miles, seemingly connecting the "pyramids" together.(127)

Figure 91: Dr. Sam Semir Osmanagich giving a tour of Ravne Underground Tunnel Labyrinth, Bosnian Pyramids, 8-13-2015

According to Dr. Osmanagic, it was clear from the very start of the excavation that all of the side tunnels were closed off by stone walls, filled up, and sealed with river bed material. It took workers a lot of time and effort to remove the debris and fill material, to reveal what was inside.(128)

To the amazement of the locals and the media, an extensive area of subterranean construction was discovered. This directly led to an enthusiastic flurry of archeological activity at the Bosnian Pyramids and nearby surrounding areas. Since being first publicized in 2005, there has been an increase in people volunteering to clean and secure additional entrances to the prehistoric tunnel network.(130)

Boston University's Curtis Runnels, an "expert" in prehistoric Greece and the Balkans, declared that the ancient builders of the Bosnian site were not capable of building on such a large scale. According to Dr. Runnels: "These people did not have the tools or skills to engage in the construction of monumental architecture."(129)

Despite the expected skepticism from federally funded mainstream anthropologists, volunteers continue to expose more of the ancient concrete on the surface of the pyramids, connecting two archaeological trenches at what is called the Bosnian Pyramid of the Sun.(130) Considering the amount of progress that has been made since excavation began, the volunteers should be commended for the time and effort that went into clearing the access paths to the Pyramid, as well as to the labyrinth below it.

The Bosnian Pyramid of the Sun is approximately one third taller than the Great Pyramid at Giza. According to Dr. Osmanagic, it was constructed with five thick layers of concrete (sandstone slabs, almost one meter thick each), with a 15 centimeter layer of clay in between each of the layers. Underneath the concrete and clay, the inner portion consists of sandstone blocks.(128)

A breakthrough discovery was made in 2012, when a team of volunteers led by the Italian archaeologists, Dr. Riccardo Brett and Niccolo Bisconti, found a fossilized leaf on top of one of the sandstone blocks. The radiocarbon dating lab in Kiev showed that the leaf is about 24,800 years old.(129) This evidence potentially shows the earliest age of the pyramidal structure.

When the Bosnian Pyramid of the Sun was first discovered in 2005, researchers estimated its age by measuring the age of the topsoil covering it.

The radiocarbon measurements showed that the topsoil is up to 12,000 years old.(129) The carbon dating of the fossilized leaf sheds new light onto the true age of this European site. If the leaf is 25,000+ years old, this implies that the construction was carried out by one of the oldest civilizations known, stretching into the Pleistocene (ice age).

The process of debris cleanup and wall support will likely last several more years before the Pyramid of the Sun is reached. The workers and volunteers have already secured, cleaned, and illuminated about 600 meters of the underground network.(129)

The network of underground tunnels were discovered under the complex in Visoko at depths ranging between 5-25 meters. On average, the height of the tunnels is 3 meters and the width is 2.5 meters. The labyrinth consists of passages and chambers spreading across several kilometers, and the distance from the tunnel entrance to the Pyramid of the Sun is approximately 3 kilometers.(129)

Figure 92: Subterranean tunnels beneath the Bosnian site

Visitors can now explore the tunnels at will, with an additional 400 meters of tunnel cleared up and being secured.(130) The air circulation in the tunnel system is extremely good, because of the difference in ceiling heights throughout the network; these height variations cause differences in air pressure and natural ventilation. The slope of the tunnels is 1.5 degrees, which enables proper water drainage.

Samples of two types of mineral drip stones, stalactites and stalagmites, were found in the underground tunnels and sent to leading European laboratories for radiocarbon dating and analysis. The Radiocarbon Laboratories of Universities of Uppsala in Sweden, University of Kiel in Germany and the University of Technology in Gliwice, Poland all estimated the age of the stalagmites at more than 5,000 years old, meaning that they estimated that the underground tunnels are older than 5,000 years.(129) Are the builders of these underground tunnels the same people who built the surface structures? Maybe, but not necessarily.

Figure 93: Prehistoric Underground Bosnian Pyramid Labyrinth

Several cultures have used these underground tunnels. Remnants of a fireplace were found near the tunnel entrance, and samples of organic material from it were sent to Sweden and Poland for radiocarbon analysis, which displayed an age of 3,000+ years.(129) At some point, some of the side tunnels and chambers spawning from the main tunnel had been closed with rocks, pebbles, sand and clay and sealed with drywall. The radiocarbon analysis of the material used to close the chambers is younger than the tunnels are estimated to be.(129) Workers are currently opening the chambers and side tunnels, as well as cleaning up the material used for sealing.

Seven leading European archaeologists issued a European Association of Archaeologists Declaration, stating:

◇◇

"We, the undersigned professional archaeologists from all parts of Europe, wish to protest strongly at the continuing support by the

Bosnian authorities for the so-called "pyramid" project being conducted on hills at and near Visoko. This scheme is a cruel hoax on an unsuspecting public and has no place in the world of genuine science. It is a waste of scarce resources that would be much better used in protecting the genuine archaeological heritage and is diverting attention from the pressing problems that are affecting professional archaeologists in Bosnia-Herzegovina on a daily basis."(128)

◇◇

The Declaration was signed by Hermann Parzinger, President of German Archaeological Institute in Berlin, Willem Willems, Inspector General of Rijksinspectie Archeologie in The Hague, Jean-Paul Demoule, President of the Institut national de recherches archéologiques préventives (INRAP) in Paris, Romuald Schild, Director of the Institute of Archaeology and Ethnology of the Polish Academy of Sciences in Warsaw, Vassil Nikolov, Director of the Institute of Archaeology of the Bulgarian Academy of Sciences in Sofia, Anthony Harding, President of the European Association of Archaeologists, and Mike Heyworth, Director of the Council for British Archaeology in York.(128)

For now, the Bosnian archeological site remains officially the stuff of legends. That said, legends of an advanced civilization of 'gods,' who built vast underground cities as refuges and shelter from the violence or cataclysmic events on the surface, appear in the mythology of numerous cultures separated by great distances; from China and Eurasia to the New World.(48)

Perhaps the thousands of subterranean tunnels, deep underground caves, and connected cavern networks can best be explained by these largely ignored "myths". Exactly what were these extensive underground dwellings used for, why were they originally built, and by whom remains a mystery, but one that may see light at the end of the tunnel during our lifetime.

Las Cuevas de Nerja (the Caves of Nerja) are an elaborate series of naturally formed caves and caverns in the hills of Maro, Spain. Located just 4km North-East of Nerja, some of these caves are said to have taken up to two million years to form.(138) They contain the widest naturally-formed column known in the world, at 32m high and 13x7m at its base. Formed by the merging of a stalagmite and a stalactite, the Caves of Nerja have held the Guinness World Record since 1989.

Figure 94: Las Cuevas de Nerja (Caves of Nerja) Maro, Spain

Stretching over 3 miles (about 5 km), these caverns are a major tourist attraction. The site is steeped in both geological and archaeological interest; cave paintings depict goats, horses, seals and birds, in red and black pigments. These enormous caves have surprisingly easy access, via a flight of stairs and concreted pathways, to allow tourists to move easily about.

In February 2012, it was announced that Neanderthal cave paintings had been discovered in the Caves of Nerja. These paintings have been radiocarbon dated to between 43,500 and 42,300 years old.(139) If this dating holds true, then it suggests that the paintings may be substantially older than the 30,000-year-old Chauvet cave paintings in south-east France, thought to be the earliest example of Palaeolithic cave art.(48) This is a big deal in the world of anthropology, as no permanent cave art has previously been attributed to our Neanderthal "cousins".

The Skocjan cave system in Slovenia includes the highest cave hall in Europe, featuring a massive underground gorge with a waterfall, and a bridge over the gorge that looks like something out of the movie, *The Lord of the Rings*. The caves have beautiful stalactite and stalagmite structures, which resemble melted wax.

Figure 95: Skocjan Caves are a huge underground labyrinth of over six kilometers of underground caverns and passages

The Skocjan Caves were formed by the sinking Reka River. The river remains on the surface at the cave entrance, but suddenly disappears underground, where it continues its way through the underground caverns. The river emerges on the surface again, not far from the Adriatic coast, after flowing underground for about 21 miles.(132)

Entered on UNESCO's list of natural and cultural world heritage sites in 1986, the Skocjan Caves represent the most significant underground phenomena in both the Karst region and Slovenia, and one of the largest underground canyons in the world.(133) A special ecosystem has developed in these caves due to particular micro-climatic conditions.(131)

Figure 96: Entrance hall to the Skocjan Caves, Slovenia

The Skocjan Caves have great cultural, historical, and national significance, as the location has been inhabited by modern humans since the Late Pleistocene.(132) The exceptional volume of the underground canyon is what distinguishes it from other cave systems, and places the archeological site among the most memorable underground tourist destinations in the world.

The river flowing through the underground canyon is approximately 3.5 km long, 10 to 60 m wide and over 140 m high, expanding into huge underground chambers. The largest of these is Martel's Chamber, with a volume of 2.2 million cubic meters, making it one of the largest discovered underground chambers in the world.(133)

In 2009, *Transylvanian Sunrise* was published, chronicling a discovery made below the "Romanian Sphinx," a site at an altitude of 2216 meters in the Bucegi Mountains of Romania.(124) Under the naturally eroded stone megalith which, depending on the angle, resembles an eroded sphinx-like structure, there is rumored to be a tunnel entrance leading into the bowels of the Earth.(124)

Figure 97: The Romanian Sphinx. Bucegi Mountains, Romania.

Babele (meaning: old women) is the local Romanian name for an area on the Bucegi Mountain plateau, only a 10 minute walk from the Romanian Sphinx. One of the most popular tourist destinations in the country, it gets its name from the mushroom shaped rock formations that are found there, which are the result of erosion.(124)

Figure 98: Babele on the Bucegi Mountains plateau in Romania

There are at least three main tunnels referred to in *Transylvanian Sunrise,* one of which leads to the underground caverns.(124) In one of the caverns, there are over-sized stone tables which stand two meters in height. They give the impression of having served people obviously much taller than we are. The book has been well received, but largely written off as fiction. That said, interest has increasingly grown since its publication, especially surrounding the parts of the story concerning giants and their subterranean habitat.

Figure 99: (Left) Monastery at the entrance of Ialomitei Cave in the Bucegi Mountains, Romania (Right) View inside the cave

The Ialomitei cave in the Romania, near the border of Transylvania, is said to have mysterious tunnels which lead into areas not accessible to the tourists who come to visit the Monastery which guards one of the caves. Could Romania be another entry point to the world below? Some claim the answer is yes, and suggest that the Romanian Intelligence Service (Department Zero) conspire to keep it hidden.(124)

If entrances to subterranean worlds exist in Romania, or in other parts of the world, then why keep them a secret? A better question might be: who benefits from keeping discoveries pertaining to the inner Earth shrouded in secrecy?

Having been academically educated in anthropology, I have formally concluded that the accepted model for human origins, popularly referred to by the media as the "out-of-Africa" replacement theory, is unambiguously false.(58) The recent sequencing of the Human genome, as well as current discoveries made in the hominid fossil record, have firmly established - at least in my mind - that we are all, in fact, members of a hybridized species.(58)

Since the end of WW2, organizations with globalist agendas, such as the United Nations, have disseminated politically correct egalitarian propaganda, insisting that a single, genetically mutated, hominid race emerged from Africa. No credible scientific evidence adequately supports this obsolete hypothesis, despite the seemingly endless funding and media attention it receives.(58) In ancient cultures around the world, one never finds legends or myths about people descending from apes. In fact, the opposite is the case in many cultures, for example the Maya:

"The Second world, or sun, was governed by Quetzalcoatl, and the earth was populated by humans. This world came to an end through hurricanes and floods. The survivors fled to the top of the trees and were transformed into monkeys."(149)

So, if we did not come down from the trees, could it be instead that we emerged from below? The introduction to this book attempts to establish the point that sunlight is not necessary for photosynthesis, nor for the chain of life to be established. The oxygen we breathe comes primarily from aquatic organisms, many of which thrive near deep underwater vents, including some species which are bioluminescent. In light of these facts, it seems entirely plausible that not only do civilizations survive comfortably underground, but that they might have originated there as well.

If they exist, the obvious advantages afforded to such sheltered subterranean civilizations, given the periodic cataclysmic events which devastate the surface population, makes conspiracy theories regarding underground over-lords suspiciously likely. Could it be that the inner world not only holds the answers to our ancient origins, but also to some of the mythological races some ancient cultures perceived as "gods"?

Figure 100: Robert Sepehr, Pergamon Museum, Berlin, Germany

If life did have its genesis inside our planet's interior, rather than from a solar based food chain, the implication is that life, and possibly intelligent life, could begin in just the same way inside other planets and moons, without the ideal surface conditions we have been told are an absolute requirement. We already know that Mars has water, so if this theory holds true, it may be just a matter of time before we hear the announcement that it also has life.

Bibliography

1. Walker, J. C. G. (1980) The oxygen cycle in the natural environment and the biogeochemical cycles, Springer-Verlag, Berlin, Germany

2. Round, F E (1981). The Ecology of Algae. London: Cambridge University Press.

3. "The Discovery of Hydrothermal Vents - 25th Anniversary CD-ROM" ©2002 Woods Hole Oceanographic Institution

4. Baker, Edward T.; Massoth, Gary J.; Feely, Richard A. (1987). "Cataclysmic hydrothermal venting on the Juan de Fuca Ridge". Nature 329: 149–151.

5. Fischman, Josh (March 1, 1999). "In Search of Megaplumes". Discover Magazine. Retrieved 18 February 2012.

6. Elton, C. S. (1927). Animal Ecology. London, UK.: Sidgwick and Jackson.

7. Fitzpatrick, Garret, "Earth Life May Have Originated at Deep-Sea Vents", Astrobiology Magazine, January 25, 2013

8. Went, Rachel, "NASA Hopes to Rely on Algae and Bacteria for Oxygen Production on Mars", Science Times, May 2015

9. Iacurci, Jenna, "Vast Underwater Ocean Trapped Beneath Earth's Crust", Nature World News, Jun 13, 2014

10. Pensoft Publishers. "Cave dwelling nettle discovered in China." ScienceDaily. ScienceDaily, 28 December 2012.

11. Alex Monro, Y.G. Wei, C.J. Chen. Three new species of Pilea (Urticaceae) from limestone karst in China. PhytoKeys, 2012; 19 (0): 51 DOI: 10.3897/phytokeys.19.3968

12. David C. Culver, and Tanja Pipan. (2009) The Biology of Caves and Other Subterranean Habitats. Oxford, UK: Oxford University Press.

13. Van Dover, Cindy Lee. (2000) The Ecology of Deep-Sea Hydrothermal Vents. Princeton University Press

14. Franko, D. A., and Heath, R. T. (1982). "UV-sensitive complex phosphorus: Association with dissolved humic material and iron in a bog lake," Limnol. Oceanogr. 27, 564-569.

15. David Grimaldi, Michael S. Engel, (2005), Evolution of the Insects. Cambridge University Press

16. Carol Lalli, Timothy R. Parsons. (1997) Biological Oceanography: An Introduction. Butterworth-Heinemann

17. "How do fireflies light up?" Science.howstuffworks.com (19 January 2001).

18. Etelvino J.H. Bechara. Cell. Bioluminescence: A Fungal Nightlight with an Internal Timer. Volume 25, Issue 7, pR283–R285, 30 March 2015

19. Dunlap, J.C. et al. Circadian Control Sheds Light on Fungal Bioluminescence. Cell. Volume 25, Issue 7, p964–968, 30 March 2015

20. Audrey LCC, Desjardin DE, Tan Y-S, Musa Md Y, Sabaratnam V. (2015). "Bioluminescent fungi from Peninsular Malaysia—a taxonomic and phylogenetic overview". Fungal Diversity 70 (1): 149-187.

21. Moore D, Robson GD, Trinci APF. (2011). *21st Century Guidebook to Fungi*. Cambridge, UK: Cambridge University Press. p. 246.

22. H. P. Lovecraft (Author), S. T. Joshi (Editor), (2013) The Ancient Track: The Complete Poetical Works of H. P. Lovecraft, Hippocampus Press

23. Twain, Mark, (1884) "Adventures of Huckleberry Finn (Tom Sawyer's comrade) HathiTrust Digital Library. HathiTrust.

24. "What is a lichen?, Australian National Botanical Garden". Retrieved 10 October 2014.

25. Emmerich R, Giez I, Lange OL, Proksch P. (1993). "Toxicity and antifeedant activity of lichen compounds against the polyphagous herbivorous insect Spodoptera littoralis". Phytochemistry 33 (6): 1389–94.

26. Genest, Michele . (2014). The Boreal Feast: A Culinary Journey through the North. Harbour Publishing

27. Richard Vines (30 April 2012). "Noma Keeps World's Best Restaurant Title, Fat Duck Sinks". Bloomberg. Retrieved 30 April 2012.

28. Warren, William Fairfield. (1885) *Paradise Found: The Cradle of the Human Race at the North Pole.*

29. Plato, Critias, section 114a, 360 BC

30. Bal Gangadhar Tilak. (1903) *The Arctic Home in the Vedas.*

31. Mangerud, J.; Ehlers, J.; Gibbard, P., ed. (2004). Quaternary Glaciations : Extent and Chronology 1: Part I Europe. Amsterdam: Elsevier.

32. Mueller, Tom (May 2009). "Ice Baby". nationalgeographic.com. National Geographic Society.

33. Bernard, Raymond. (1964) The Hollow Earth. Health Research WA

34. Emerson, Willis George. (1908) *A Voyage to the Inner Earth.* (The Smoky God).

35. Huanxiang Yuan, Libing Liu, Fengting Lva and Shu Wang. "Bioluminescence as a light source for photosynthesis". Chem. Commun., Sep 2013

36. O. Pes, A. Midlik, J. Schlaghamersky, M. Zitnan and P. Taborsky. "A study on bioluminescence and photoluminescence in the earthworm Eisenia lucens". Photochem. Photobiol. Sci., 2016,15, 175-180

37. Mercator, Gerardus (1554), *Declaratio insigniorum utilitatum quae sunt in globo terrestri : coelesti, et annulo astronomico ad invictissimum romanum imperatorem Carolum Quintum.* Duisberg. Reprinted in 1868 with a commentary by Jean van Raemdonck.

38. Mercator, Gerardu; Karrow, Jr., Robert W. (1570) *Atlas sive Cosmographica Meditationes de Fabrica Mundi et Fabricati Figura.* Library of Congress.

39. Uvarov, Valery. *The Second Birth of Hyperborea.*

40. Sepehr, Robert. (2015) *Species with Amnesia: Our Forgotten History.* Atlantean Gardens, USA.

41. Murrin, John M; Johnson, Paul E; McPherson, James M; Gerstle, Gary (2008). Liberty, Equality, Power: A History of the American People, Compact. Thomson Wadsworth.

42. Lankford, George E. (2011) *Native American Legends of the Southeast: Tales from the Natchez, Caddo, Biloxi, Chickasaw, and Other Nations.* University Alabama Press

43. Tate, Peter. (2011) *Flights of Fancy: Birds in Myth, Legend, and Superstition.* New York: Random House.

44. Habig, Marion, (1959) "Blessed Odoric Matiussi of Pordenone", The Franciscan Book of Saints, Franciscan Herald Press

45. The Sacred Books of China: The Texts of Confucianism. Part I The Shu King, the Religious Portions of the Shih King, the Hsiao King, trans. James Legge (Oxford: Clarendon Press, 1879)

46. Antoninus Liberalis Transformationum congeries, 1676

47. Aristotle, History of Animals, Book 8:2

48. The Circle of Ancient Iranian Studies. (2005) CAIS ARCHAEOLOGICAL & CULTURAL NEWS. (cais-soas.com)

49. Westaway, Michel Carrington; Durband, Arthur C. C; Groves, Colin P.; Collard, Mark (February 17, 2015). "Mandibular evidence supports Homo floresiensis as a distinct species". Proceedings of the National Academy of Sciences

50. Charles Q. Choi, 2010, "Giant Storks May Have Fed On Real Hobbits". Live Science

51. Meijer and Due (2010). "A new species of giant marabou stork (Ave: Ciconiiformes) from the Pleistocene of Liang Bua, Flores (Indonesia)". Zoological Journal of the Linnean Society 160: 707–724.

52. Sawyer, Susanna; Renaud, Gabriel; Viola, Bence; Hublin, Jean-Jacques; Gansauge, Marie-Theres; Shunkov, Michael V.; Derevianko, Anatoly P.; Prüfer, Kay; Kelso, Janet; Pääbo, Svante (11 November 2015). "Nuclear and mitochondrial DNA sequences from two Denisovan individuals". PNAS.

53. Hapgood, Charles H. (1966) Maps of the ancient sea kings: evidence of advanced civilization in the ice age. Adventures Unlimited Press

54. Wilson, James Grant; Fiske, John, eds. (1900). "Neuville, Philippe Buache de la". Appletons' Cyclopædia of American Biography. New York: D. Appleton.

55. Tony K. Meunier, Richard S. Williams, Jr., and Jane G. Ferrigno. "U.S. Geological Survey Scientific Activities in the Exploration of Antarctica: Introduction to Antarctica" (Including USGS Field Personnel: 1946–59)

56. Beaglehole, J.C., ed. (1968). *The Journals of Captain James Cook on His Voyages of Discovery. I: The Voyage of the Endeavour 1768-1771*. Cambridge University Press.

57. Murphy, Thomas David. (2002) *German Exploration of the Polar World: A History, 1870-1940*

58. Sepehr, Robert. (2015) *Species with Amnesia: Our Forgotten History*. Atlantean Gardens. USA

59. Friedrich, Christof. (1976) *Secret Nazi Polar Expeditions*. Samisdat

60. Sepehr, Robert. (2015). *Occult Secrets of Vril*. Atlantean Gardens. USA.

61. MI5 staff (2011). "Hitler's last days". Her Majesty's Security Service website. Retrieved 1 October 2013.

62. Summerhayes, C. & Beeching, P. "Hitler's Antarctic base: the myth and the reality". Polar Record

63. *El Mercurio*. March 5, 1947.

64. Mullins, Eustice. (1992, second edition) The World Order: Our Secret Rulers. Ezra Pound Institute of Civilization. USA

65. Salla, Michael E. (2015) Insiders Reveal Secret Space Programs & Extraterrestrial Alliances. Exopolitics Institute

66. Madden, E. F. (October 1882). "Symmes and His Theory". Harper's New Monthly Magazine (New York, NY: Harper and Bros) 65 (389): 740–744.

67. Symmes' Circular No. 1, 1818

68. Griffin, Duane (2012), "What Curiosity in the Structure: The Hollow Earth in Science" (PDF), in Berressem, Hanjo

69. Wilkins, Harold. (1946) *Mysteries of Ancient South America.*

70. Bernard, Raymond. (1964) *The Hollow Earth.* Health Research; 2nd edition

71. Huni, Carl. (1960), "The Mysterious Tunnels and Subterranean Cities of South America"

72. Leith, John. (1980) *Genesis for the New Age.*

73. Makusipe Komanto Iseru: Sustaining Makushi way of life. (1996). North Rupununi District Development Board

74. Roth, Walter E. (1915) An Inquiry into the Animism and Folk-Lore of the Guiana Indians

75. Whitehead, Neil L. (2002) Dark Shamans: Kanaima and the Poetics of Violent Death. Duke University Press Books

76. Ryan, Carolyne. *European Travel Writings and the Patagonian Giants.* Lawrence University. Retrieved August 15, 2005.

77. Munday, Anthony. The Famous and Renowned Historie of Primaleon of Greece, 1619, cap.XXXIII: "How Primaleon··· found the Grand Patagon ".

78. Pigafetta, Antonio. *Magellan's Voyage: A Narrative Account of the First Circumnavigation*, trans. R. A. Skelton (New Haven, Conn., 1969), 1:46–47, 50.

79. Murdie et al. 1999, Geo-Marine Letters 18:315-320.

80. Lovgren, Stefan (2007-04-06). "Giant crystal cave's mystery solved". National Geographic News.

81. Christopher Vecsey. The Emergence of the Hopi People, in American Indian Quarterly, vol. 7, no. 3, American Indian Religions, 70 (Summer 1983).

82. Harold Courlander. The Fourth World of the Hopis: The Epic Story of the Hopi Indians as Preserved in their Legends and Traditions, 201 (University of New Mexico Press, 1987)

83. *The Arizona Gazette.* April 5, 1909

84. *The Arizona Gazette.* March 12, 1909

85. Los Angeles Times, January 29, 1934. "Lizard People's Catacomb City Hunted Engineer Sinks Shaft Under Fort Moore Hill to Find Maze of Tunnels and Priceless Treasures of Legendary Inhabitants. By: Jean Bosquet

86. Vickie Carson (February 15, 2013). "Mammoth Cave hits 400 miles". National Park Service (NPS).

87. Meloy, Harold (Meloy 1968) Mummies of Mammoth Cave: An account of the Indian mummies discovered in Short Cave, Salts Cave, and Mammoth Cave, Kentucky Shelbyville, Indiana: Micron Publishing Co., 1990 (Original copyright 1968, 1977).

88. Watson, Patty Jo (ed.) (Watson 1974) Archaeology of the Mammoth Cave Area. Reprinted 1997 by St. Louis: Cave Books

89. H.P. Lovecraft. *The Beast in the Cave*, 1918

90. Brockington, John (2003). "The Sanskrit Epics". In Flood, Gavin. Blackwell companion to Hinduism. Blackwell Publishing

91. Buck, William; van Nooten, B. A. (2000). Ramayana. University of California Press.

92. Mott, Michael. (2000) "The Deep Dwellers"

93. Angami NagaBrown, Account of Munnipore, 1968, p. 113

94. Steiger, Brad. "The Hollow Earth: Myth or Reality". *Atlantis Rising*

95. "Guilin Reed Flute Cave". City of Guilin. Archived from the original on 20 May 2011.

96. "History of the Great Cave of Niah". *ABC Online*. Retrieved 6 January 2014.

97. World's second-largest cave to boost tourism: *The National*, May 17, 2008

98. Majlis Al Jinn Cave. Public Authority for Water Resources, Sultanate of Oman: Report PAWR 85-20, October 1985

99. Lebanese Ministry of Environment. "Lebanon State of the Environment Report" (PDF). Lebanese Ministry of Environment. Archived from the original (.pdf) on October 5, 2007.

100. Blavatsky, H.P. (1888) *Secret Doctrine 2:502-503*

101. Blavatsky, H.P. (1888) *Secret Doctrine 2:636-637*

102. Blavatsky, H.P. (1888) *Secret Doctrine 2:416*

103. *Theosophical Glossary p. 287*

104. Editorial Appendix, The Theosophist, Jan 1882, published in H.P. Blavatsky Theosophical Articles 3:333

105. Louis, PF. "Massive cave discovered in China has its own weather system". Natural news. October 14, 2013

106. Burroughs, Edgar Rice. (1914) *At the Earth's Core*. Worldcat.

107. Burroughs, Edgar Rice. (1917) Tarzan *At the Earth's Core*. Worldcat.

108. Richard Hinckley Allen. (1899) *In Star Names and Their Meanings.*

109. Krupp. E. C. "The Sphinx Blinks. The familiar stone lion with a human head that peers out over the Nile was built in adoration of the Sun." Sky & Telescope. March 2001 Issue Vol. 101 No. 3

110. Hurtak,J.J. *The Keys of Enoch.* Library of Congress 76-55939

111. Herodotus (1987). The History, translated by David Grene. University of Chicago Press

112. On the mysteries (De mysteriis), ed. Gustav Parthey, Teubner, 1857, ed. Edouard des Places, Collection Budé, 1989

113. Phillipson, David. Ancient Churches of Ethiopia (New Haven: Yale University Press, 2009)

114. Francisco Alvarez, The Prester John of the Indies, translated by C.F. Beckingham and G.W.B. Huntingford (Cambridge: Hakluyt Society, 1961), p. 226. Beckingham and Huntingford added an appendix that discusses Alvarez's description of these churches, pp. 526–42.

115. Credo Mutwa. *The SPECTRUM.* Newspaper by Rick Martin (no longer in print) 9/30/99

116. Icke, David. The Biggest Secret: The Book That Will Change the World (1999)

117. Verne, Jules. *Journey to the Center of the Earth* (1864)

118. Gardner, Marshall. (1920) *A Journey to the Earth's Interior*

119. Wolmark, Nina. *Spartakus and the Sun Beneath the Sea. (French: Les Mondes Engloutis, "The Engulfed Worlds").* French animated series. (2000)

120. Schulz, Matthias. *SPIEGEL International.* "Hideouts or Sacred Spaces? Experts Baffled by Mysterious Underground Chambers". July 22, 2011. Translated from the German by Christopher Sultan.

121. Holloway, April. (2014) "Extensive Ancient Underground Networks Discovered Throughout Europe"

122. Rossella Lorenzi. "First Ever Etruscan Pyramids Found in Italy" 2012.

123. De Grummond and Nancy Thomson (2006). Etruscan Mythology, Sacred History and Legend: An Introduction. University of Pennsylvania Museum of Archeology.

124. Moon, Peter. Cinamar, Radu. (2009) *Transylvanian Sunrise*. Sky Books

125. Berger, Lee R.; et al. (10 September 2015). "Homo naledi, a new species of the genus Homo from the Dinaledi Chamber, South Africa". eLife

126. Bradshaw, William Richard. (1892) *The Goddess of Atvatabar*.

127. Tara MacIsaac (13 November 2013). "5 Mysterious Ruins That Predate Known Civilization?". The Epoch Times.

128. Mark Rose, Bosnian "Pyramids" Update, Archaeology Magazine Online, 14 June 2006

129. Carolyn Khew (14 August 2015). "Pyramids exist in Bosnia: Archaeologist". The Straits Times.

130. bosnianpyramids.org

131. Andrej Kranjc: *Historical overview and description of the caves*, pages 42-57

132. Turk, Peter. *Archeology*, pages: 86-97

133. Skocjan Caves - Description. UNESCO World Heritage Centre.

134. *Amazing Stories magazine*, pp. 171-172. (Oct 1947)

135. "Creation of Carlsbad Cave National Monument". National Park Service. Retrieved 2012-07-13.

136. *AMAZING STORIES* magazine (Jan 1948)

137. Browne, Malcom W. "Underground Tunnels Threaten Town in Hungary's Wine Country". NEW YORK TIMES, Nov. 8, 1967, p.2

138. Oldham, Tony. "Cueva de Nerja". Retrieved 6 June 2007

139. Fergal MacErlean. "First Neanderthal cave paintings discovered in Spain" New scientist. February 10, 2012

140. Brugger, Karl. (1977) *The Chronicle of Akakor.* Abe Books.

141. Chaney, Earlyne. "Odyssey Into Egypt". (May, 1982) VOICE OF ASTARA.

142. Greene, Vaughn. Issue No. 14 of *The Shaver Mystery Club Letterzine.*

143. NATIONAL ENQUIRER., Feb. 4., 1973 pp. 16-17

144. Hall, Manly P. (1932) *Man: Grand Symbol of the Mysteries: Thoughts In Occult Anatomy.* Manly P. Hall Pub. Co., Los Angeles, CA, 1932, p. 160

145. Rojas, Victoria. *Reuters.* "Portal to mythical Mayan underworld found in Mexico". Aug 15, 2008

146. Braun, Kirt. '*BEYOND REALITY*' (Dec. 1968)

147. Spiro Kostof, *Caves of God: Cappadocia and its Churches* Publisher: Oxford University Press, 1989

148. Tomas, Andrew. (1974) *On the Shores of Endless Worlds.* (chapter "Labyrinths and Serpents"). Souvenir Press

149. Van Tuerenhout, Dirk R. (2005) *The Aztecs: New Perspectives.*

Images

1) Drawing showing examples of red, brown, and green algae.

2) Juan de Fuca Ridge hydrothermal vent "back smoker"

3) Juan de Fuca Ridge sea spider

4) An artist's concept of greenhouses on Mars. Image: NASA

5) An artistic depiction of a subterranean river.

6) Dr. Charlotte Marcinko of the National Oceanography Center demonstrating how bioluminescent organisms react (glow) when stimulated.

7) Light bulb that uses bioluminescent bacteria to generate light without any electrical input.

8) Boat tour of the Waitomo Caves, New Zealand

9) Bioluminescent mushrooms found in the forests of Sao Paulo, Brazil

10) Bioluminescent mushrooms found on the Bonin Islands near the coast of Japan.

11) Glowing bioluminescent mushrooms.

12) Edible lichen.

13) Image from Noma, a Danish restaurant in Copenhagen that serves moss and lichen

14) Scanned image of William Fairfield Warren (1833-1929)

15) Scanned image of Bal Gangadhar Tilak (1856-1920)

16) Preserved carcass of baby mammoth.

17)   Sailboat seen through iceberg.

18-1)   Snanned image of the arctic map from the Theatrum Orbis Terrarum by Abraham Ortelius (1570)

18-2)   Scanned image of Gerardus Mercator (1512-1594)

19)   Gerardus Mercator's map of the Arctic (1569)

20)   The center portion of Gerardus Mercator's map of the Arctic (1569)

21)   Scanned detail from the Carta Marina map by Olaus Magnus (1539)

22)   Battle of Pygmies and Cranes from a vase found at Pompeii. Harper's Dictionary of Classical Antiquities.

23)   Sketch of art from the Francois vase (570 BC) depicting the battle between Pygmy and Crane. Museum of Florence.

24)   Leptis Magna 6th Century AD. Cranes vs Pygmies Villa Silene.

25)   Pygmies ride she-goats into battle. Carta Marina map by Olaus Magnus (1539)

26)   4th Century Etruscan vase painting showing a Pygmy striking a large Crane's neck

27)   Nurenburg Chronicle (1493) Pygmy battling Cranes

28)   Museum Collection: State Hermitage Museum, St Petersburg, Russia. Etruscan, 4th Century

29)   Capital column, Autun cathedral, Saone-et-Loire department, Burgundy, France

30-a)   Greek vase (430 BC) National Archeological Museum of Spain

30-b)   Kerman province near Shahdad city, Iran

31)   Homo floresiensis skull next to modern Holocene Homo sapien skull

32)   Artist depiction of giant stork next to Homo floresiensis or "Hobbit"

33)   Artist depiction of Pleistocene Hominids

34) Sketch drawing of giant stork carrying "Hobbit"

35) Statue of admiral Piri Reis and his 1513 map in the background

36) Oronteus Finaeus map (1531) of Antarctica free of ice.

37) Philippe Buache's world map (1737)

38) SS Schwabenland and badge of the German Antarctic Expedition (1938-39)

39) Crew of the 1938-39 German Antarctic Expedition

40) German map showing Neuschwabenland

41) German U-boat (submarine)

42) Ladies of the Vril Society

43) Admiral Doenitz and Adolf Hitler

44) Haunebu series disc craft, Germany

45) Admiral Byrd Antarctic Expedition stamps

46) Documents allegedly showing the SS U-boat route to Agartha, Inner Earth

47) Modified globe to show Inner Earth as described by Symmes

48-a) Image of Inner Earth polar entrance in Harper's New Monthly Magazine (1882)

48-b) The Hollow Earth Hypothesis, from The Goddess of Atvatabar, 1892.

49) Drawing of Lost City of Z, as described by Col. Percy Harrison

50-a) Native people of Manau, Brazil. (1895) Photo: George Huebner

50-b) Unusually tall man from an indigenous tribe in Brazil. Photo by Orlando Villas Boas.

51-a) Map drawing of the Amazon river in South America

51-b) Archeologists Victoria Rojas (front) and Lara Hindersten (back) work at a site at the village of Tahtzibichen in Merida, Yucatan

Peninsula, April 12, 2008. REUTERS / Team of investigators / Tammara Thomsen/Handout

51-c)   Tikal, Guatemala, 4th Century BC

52)   Map by Diego Gutierrez (1562) showing Patagonian Giants

53)   Dom Pernety (1771)

54)   A Voyage Around the World (1767)

55-a)   Marble caves, Patagonia, Chile

55-b)   Cave of Crystals. Naico, Chihuahua, Mexico

56)   Cave of Crystals. Naico, Chihuahua, Mexico

57-a)   Grand Canyon, Arizona

57-b)   The Arizona Gazette April 5, 1909

58)   La Times (1934) Map of Los Angeles underground tunnels

59)   Mammoth Cave, Kentucky

60)   Echo River 360 feet below ground. Mammoth Cave, Kentucky

61)   Carlsbad Caverns, New Mexico

62)   Karnataka, India. Naga stone sculptures

63)   Flute Reed Cave, China

64)   Flute Reed Cave Stalactites and Stalagmites. China

65)   The Great Cave of Niah, Malaysia

66)   Inside the Great Cave of Niah, Malaysia

67)   Puerto Princesa Underground River

68)   Puerto Princesa Underground River, Philippines

69)   Tourist boat ride into the Puerto Princesa Underground River, Philippines

70)   Majlis as Jinn (Arabic: "meeting place of the Jinn")

71)   Majlis al Jinn cave, Oman

72)   Jeita grotto, Lebanon

73)   The Gobi Desert, China

74)   Map from *Atlantis the Antediluvian World* (1882)

75)   Map from *Species with Amnesia: Our Forgotten History* (2015)

76)   H.P. Blavatsky

77)   Er Wang Dong, Chongqing, China

78-a)   Scanned image of the Longyou Caves, China

78-b)   Scanned image of a tunnel below Derinkuyu, Turkey

78-c)   Drawing depicting the underground city at Derinkuyu, Turkey

79)   "Iron Mole" from *At the Earth's Core*

80)   *Tarzan At the Earth's Core* cover art by David B. Mattingly

81)   German blimps WWI

82)   Scanned sketch of Egyptian Pyramids and Sphinx

83)   Lalibela, Ethiopia stone carved Church

84)   Church carved below the surface out of rock. Lalibela, Ethiopia.

85)   Lalibela, Ethiopia. Church windows with swastika design.

86)   Images of Credo Mutwa of South Africa

87)   Illustrations from *Journey to the Center of the Earth* (1864)

88)   Showing the earth bisected centrally through the polar openings and at right angles to the equator, giving a clear view of the central sun and the interior continents and oceans. (Reproduced from photograph of working model.) Made by the author, 1912. Patented May 12, 1914,Gardner, Marshall. (1920) A Journey to the Earth's Interior

89)   Photos: Dr. Heinrich Kush. Underground tunnel system

90)   Orvieto, Italy. Stone structures

91) Photos: Dr. Sam Semir Osmanagich giving a tour of Ravne Underground Tunnel Labyrinth, Bosnian Pyramids, 8-13-2015

92) Photo of Tunnels below the Bosnian Valley of Pyramids.

93) Labyrinth under the Bosnian Pyramid complex

94) Scanned photo of the Nerja Caves, Spain

95) Scanned photo of Skocjan Caves, Slovenia.

96) Scanned photo of Skocjan Caves entrance. Slovenia.

97) Scanned photo of The Romanian Sphinx, Romania

98) Scanned photo of Babele on the Bucegi Mountain Plateau, Romanian

99) Scanned photo of Monastery at the Ialomitei cave, the Bucegi Mountains, Romania

100) Photo of Robert Sepehr, Pergamon Museum, Berlin, Germany

Made in the USA
San Bernardino, CA
28 January 2020